Inspiralized

Inspiralized

Turn Vegetables into Healthy,
Creative, Satisfying Meals

ALI MAFFUCCI
PHOTOGRAPHS BY EVAN SUNG

CLARKSON POTTER/PUBLISHERS
NEW YORK

Copyright © 2015 by Alissandra Maffucci
Photographs copyright © 2015 by Evan Sung

Published in the United States by Clarkson
Potter/Publishers, an imprint of the Crown
Publishing Group, a division of Random House
LLC, a Penguin Random House Company,
New York.
www.crownpublishing.com
www.clarksonpotter.com

CLARKSON POTTER is a trademark and
POTTER with colophon is a registered
trademark of Random House LLC.

Library of Congress Cataloging-in-Publication Data
Maffucci, Ali.
Inspiralized: turn vegetables into healthy,
creative, satisfying meals / Ali Maffucci ;
photographs by Evan Sung.—First edition.
1. Cooking (Vegetables) 2. Vegetable carving.
3. Grinding machines. I. Title.
TX801.M246 2015
641.6'5—dc23   2014041703

ISBN 978-0-8041-8683-4
eBook ISBN 978-0-8041-8684-1

Printed in China

Book design by Ashley Tucker
Cover design by La Tricia Watford
Cover photo by Evan Sung
Photo on page 10:
courtesy of the author
Photo on page 11:
Nadya Furnari Photography
Photos on pages 12, 33, and 213:
Unique Lapin Photography

10 9 8 7 6 5 4

First Edition

Life is a combination of magic and pasta.

—FEDERICO FELLINI

Some are born with silver spoons in their mouths, some with plastic ones, and some with none. All I know is that my spoon was definitely dripping with tomato-basil sauce.

This book is dedicated to my Italian-American grandparents, who brought love and joy into our family through food. Thank you for making cooking and, most of all, eating so much fun.

Special dedication to:

Mom, for your undying support, love, and faith in me.

Dad, for teaching me to work hard for what I want.

Lu, for inspiring me to start *Inspiralized* and being my daily taste tester. I love you.

My Grandmother Ida, for giving me my thirst for knowledge.

My *Inspiralized* readers: Thanks to your loyal support and following, this cookbook was made possible.

And to all lovers of pasta and carbs. *Salute!*

CONTENTS

INTRODUCTION 9

Getting Inspiralized 15

Ready, Set, Spiralize! 21

Breakfasts 35

Snacks & Sides 55

Soups, Stews & Salads 75

Sandwiches, Wraps & More 101

Casseroles 121

Rice Dishes 139

Pastas & Noodles 163

Desserts 193

FRUITS AND VEGGIES, A–Z 208

ACKNOWLEDGMENTS 218

INDEX 220

If I had a dollar for every time my grandparents said, "We're on a diet—we're giving up pasta, wine, and cheese," I wouldn't be here writing this book. I'd be living on an island with my riches.

Sunday-night dinners at the home of my father's parents were always quite the scene. My sweet grandmother—a woman who proudly donned her Sunday best for Mass and washed my mouth out with soap for saying "pee" instead of "tinkle"—would be burning something in the oven and scuffling about the kitchen with a spoon in her hand, dripping sauce on the tiled floors. But despite the chaos, Pops, with his big gold pinky ring, strong nose, and all-consuming love of the motherland, always managed to prepare a flawless meatball or the perfect pesto.

Cooking was always the main event. The party didn't start when everyone arrived for dinner; it started when the first *glug* of olive oil hit the pan, signaling the beginning of a beautiful, delicious Italian meal. We were all pulled in not only by the smell of a fresh marinara simmering but also by the clinks of wineglasses filled with full-bodied reds and sounds of Pops's favorite Frank Sinatra album (if you could hear the songs over his own renditions). The sight of Pops twirling my grandmother around to "That's Amore" is unforgettable.

Eating was another spectacle. My father would fight anyone for the last piece of bread to dip in the sauce left on his plate—God forbid we didn't savor every last drop. The wine flowed, and my grandmother constantly got up to bring something else to the table, whether olive oil, more bread, or freshly grated Parmesan. Despite conversations that could be either negative or positive, the mood was always jovial, simply because we were *eating*. We gorged ourselves on pasta, meats, wine, and cheese nearly to the point of discomfort—yet we never missed dessert. And that was always an assortment of Italian pastries from a *molto bene* bakery—biscotti, sfogliatelle, pignoli. My personal favorite was cannoli and Sambuca, the little espresso beans floating in that sweet anise-flavored liquor paired with decadent ricotta-filled pastry. By the time we left my grandparents we had eaten our weight in carbohydrates, but we were happy. My grandmother and Pops would walk us out the front door and wait to wave good-bye as we drove out the driveway. Everyone was already excited for the next Sunday.

When I had the opportunity to spend a college semester studying abroad, I of course went to Italy. I treated every day as if it were Sunday night dinner at my grandparents'. I devoured pizzas, polished off aromatic Chiantis, ripped through caprese salads, slurped up giant portions of pasta bolognese, and dipped fresh semolina bread into whatever I could get my hands on. I might as well have just slurped olive oil straight from the bottle. When I returned home, I had to face the consequences of my indulgences: high numbers on the scale. I had put on an embarassing 20 pounds during my indulgent European semester, bringing my grand total weight gain to 50 pounds since freshman year. When I saw that number, I knew something had to change.

I gave myself some leniency, as I was suffering withdrawal from *la dolce vita*, after all. Then my friend Sarah gave me a book on—are you sitting down?—veganism. Despite fear of a painful good-bye to sausage, mozzarella, thick pestos, meatballs, and white pastas and breads, I was quickly sold on the promises of slender arms and skinny thighs. In August 2008, I began a two-year stint as a vegan and it worked: I lost 60 pounds and obtained the arms and thighs of my dreams. But, there was one big problem: Sunday night dinners at my grandparents' were different—and not in a good way. Telling my family I was a vegan was like telling them I was moving to the most desolate corner of the world. Whole-grain pasta and multigrain bread just weren't part of Pops's vocabulary. Luckily, my grandparents' unconditional love prevailed, and they made extra dishes for me: more vegetables, whole wheat spaghetti, and pasta fagioli. It just wasn't the same, though.

As a result of adopting veganism, I learned how to cook creatively and healthfully, discovered new types of food, and became empowered by my knowledge of fresh, clean eating and its immense health benefits. As an Italian-American and lover of pastas and savory foods, I still struggled with portion

control—until my mother introduced me to the spiralizer. After that, my life changed.

So, how did it all start?

My mother is a Type 1 diabetic. This type of diabetes, which often begins in childhood, is known as insulin-dependent diabetes because the pancreas produces little or no insulin, a hormone that normally converts glucose (sugar) into energy. If not managed properly, this chronic diabetes can cause serious health problems, such as kidney failure, blindness, nerve damage, fatal heart disease, and stroke. Although there are many causes for diabetes, my mother initially developed gestational diabetes, becoming diabetic while pregnant. In 2012, when I was living in Hoboken, New Jersey, she started seeing a health coach who suggested she try raw veganism, a diet that excludes not only all animal products but also foods cooked above a temperature of about 118°F.

A few weeks later, on vacation in Florida, she researched raw vegan restaurants and found one nearby. She figured she would try out restaurant-quality raw food before committing to the lifestyle. She ordered a "Dragon Bowl," which listed zucchini noodles as one of its ingredients. My mother was impressed and amazed by it—so much so that she told me about the dish right away. She wanted to recreate those zucchini noodles at home, but she didn't know how.

A few months later, in New York City, we went to a raw organic restaurant called Pure Food and Wine. We had an incredible meal,

so my mother was committed to eating more vegan and plant-based foods. She bought the restaurant's cookbook, and that's when she discovered the spiralizer. One of the recipes in the book was for zucchini noodles.

My mother insisted I should try these noodles, but I was incredulous: how could a vegetable noodle taste like pasta, especially to someone who had grown up eating so much pasta? Then, one Sunday evening she made me a dish with them. I was floored. I was expecting something either crunchy and raw or mushy and overcooked, but what I tasted was the same lovely consistency of al dente pasta. Honestly, if my eyes had been closed, I would have thought she served me real spaghetti!

Always looking for new ways to eat healthfully, I was captivated. Most important, I regretted not having tried it sooner. I apologized for being so stubborn, and I thanked my mother. She sent me home with her spiralizer and bought another for herself.

I counted the hours at work the next day, eager to go home and make zucchini noodles for my dinner that night. I decided to make a tomato-basil pasta with cannellini beans, roasted artichokes, and shrimp. In just minutes, I had a pasta dish that was low-calorie, low-carb, and nutritious. And it seemed to come so naturally. Although my mother had presented the zucchini noodles as a spaghetti replacement, I saw that they had greater potential. As soon as I started turning the handle of my spiralizer, recipe ideas began filling my head.

Lu, my boyfriend at the time, had no idea what I was doing, of course. He was just hungry, as usual. When the meal was ready, I tasted the dish and knew I had something special. Lu took his first bite, threw his head back, and roared "Mmmm!"

"I know, right?" I said excitedly.

Immediately, he responded, "How come everyone doesn't know about this?"

For the next three months, all I could do was think about spiralizing. If I went to a coffee shop on the weekend, I'd bring my laptop to write recipes, and I left wanting to test them that evening. I felt this great urge to *create*. After years of working in static corporate environments, I finally had an outlet: spiralizing had inspired me! Simply put, I was *Inspiralized*, and I wanted to Inspiralize others.

The more I cooked spiralized meals, the more convinced I became of their potential. I started posting pictures of my spiralized dinners on my social media channels, and my friends commented back, asking for the recipes. When I told them the noodles were made with a spiralizer, they bought their own to get started. I was creating buzz in my own social circle, so I knew the idea would catch on just as quickly with the rest of the world.

I was especially happy to tell everyone on low-carb diets that pasta and noodle bowls could be enjoyed again, and not just on "cheat day." Like them, I was tired of green juices and boring lean proteins and veggies for dinner. I also couldn't find truly diet-friendly food that tasted great. But now I had the key to that castle!

When I searched online for "spiralized recipes," everything that turned up was raw, vegan, or both. The only recipes I could find stuck to three basic veggies: carrots, cucumbers, and zucchini. No one was capturing the true power of the spiralizer.

Finally, in June 2013, after mustering up the necessary courage, I walked into my boss's office and quit my job. Then I rushed home, bright-eyed and bushy-tailed, and purchased the domain name Inspiralized.com. That next morning, I walked into a coffee shop across the street, opened up my laptop, and without a clue as to how to start a blog, I wrote my first post and began drafting a business plan.

In order to create and test recipes that did not exclude any types of eaters, I went from vegan to pescatarian to omnivore again.

Reintroducing these favorite foods to my diet was welcomed, not feared. I took a culinary journey that allowed me to manage my waistline as I adapted all my food knowledge to this new spiralized way of cooking. My body has slimmed down, my skin glows, and I have more energy than ever before.

Most important? Sunday dinners at my grandparents' house are again satisfying and delicious.

GETTING INSPIRALIZED

Inspiralized is what your meal and *you* become—a healthy and inspired version of the original! When you work vegetable noodles and vegetable rice into your diet, you'll start to notice the effects almost instantly: glowing skin, better digestion, more energy, and overall dietary satisfaction. You will no longer crave the heavy carbs, sugars, or processed foods. Your body will be so satisfied and so well nourished that you'll forget about "real" pasta and noodles and "real" rice, and you'll yearn for more lean, whole, and clean foods. Most important, you'll want to invent your own recipes, whether that means adapting the classics and your favorites or experimenting with new ideas. You'll find yourself eager to get home and Inspiralize.

The Health Benefits

These days, *healthy* is a relative and confusing term. We've lost the concept of what's truly healthy; we place labels on strict diets that we follow instead of learning what works best for our own bodies. Of course, for some of us, strict guidelines can help keep a weight-loss journey on track or help manage an illness. Regardless of your food outlook, you'll be hard pressed to find a dietary lifestyle that doesn't advocate eating more vegetables.

When you add more vegetables to your diet, the health benefits are immense. They include:

HIGHER INTAKE OF DIETARY FIBER: The fiber in vegetables helps reduce blood cholesterol levels and therefore may lower the risk of heart disease. Dietary fiber also helps provide a feeling of fullness with fewer calories, which promotes overall weight loss and health maintenance.

MORE NUTRIENT DENSITY: Simply put, vegetables have tons of nutrients. Vitamins A and C help keep your skin healthy and your immune system strong, respectively; potassium and folate help your muscles function and your body to build cells, respectively. Overall, these nutrients keep your body running optimally and keep you feeling more energized.

DISEASE PREVENTION: Many studies prove that a diet rich in veggies and fruits slows the absorption of sugar into your bloodstream, lowering the risk of diabetes. Plus, a veggie- and fruit-rich diet prevents fatty substances from sticking to blood vessel walls, helping defend against heart disease.

Imagine if you ate a big bowl of wheat pasta, but didn't feel uncomfortable or lethargic afterward; instead of needing to lie down, you felt like going dancing or taking a walk with your dinner date. Instead of feeling guilty for indulging, you felt that you were doing something positive for your body. That's what it will be like if you eat a bowl of vegetable noodles—same great taste, but with a much better feeling afterward.

Now, I'm not suggesting that you never again eat a bowl of regular pasta or rice. Carbohydrates are a crucial part of a healthy balanced diet, and they should be eaten in their recommended daily amounts. However, they should be consumed in a whole, unprocessed manner so you can best absorb their health benefits. Adding spiralized sweet potatoes to a meal, for example, is an effective way to obtain those clean carbohydrates. But if you're at a restaurant and feel like having a bowl of spaghetti bolognese, go for it—everything in moderation, always.

Nutritional Information: Pasta Noodles vs. Vegetable Noodles

Now, let's get to the facts and figures of it all. Looking at a nutritional comparison of the most commonly spiralized vegetables and regular wheat pasta shows the stark

Pasta Noodles vs. Vegetable Noodles

	SERVING SIZE	CALORIES	CARBS	PROTEIN	FAT
Wheat Spaghetti	140 g	221	43 g	8 g	1.3 g
Carrot	190 g	77.9	19 g	1.7 g	0.4 g
Cucumber	398 g	30.4	6.84 g	1.14 g	0.19 g
Beet	150 g	64.5	15 g	2.4 g	0.3 g
Butternut squash	180 g	81	21.6 g	1.8 g	0.18 g
Kohlrabi	385 g	71.82	15.96 g	4.5 g	.27 g
Zucchini	245 g	41.7	7.6 g	2.9 g	0.7 g

differences. The chart on the opposite page shows a proper serving of vegetable noodles and the recommended serving of wheat pasta, as indicated on the box. When you eat a pasta dish at a restaurant, the quantity is often double or triple that recommended boxed serving!

All of the serving sizes for the vegetable pastas are based on a plentiful bowl of raw noodles. If cooked, they yield 1½ to 2 heaping cups of vegetable noodles. Keep in mind that there are no USDA guidelines for vegetable pasta serving sizes. These are just best practices that have been suggested, tested, and "approved" by me.

Of course, with spiralizing, you can vary and combine vegetables to obtain varied amounts of vitamins and minerals; that is, you can build meals based on your own dietary needs, which isn't possible with regular pasta and noodles. For example, those who suffer from an iron deficiency could substitute spiralized potatoes and broccoli, both high in iron. Add spinach and some beans, and you'll pack in more than enough iron in one delicious meal. Can regular pasta do that?

Daily Vegetable Intake

We're always being told to eat our vegetables. Well, if you're not a veggie lover, I have good news. By eating vegetable noodles or vegetable rice, you easily take in your daily recommended amount of veggies without it tasting like you are. Instead of begrudgingly pureeing the vegetable into a smoothie or eating it in a boring side salad, you can build

it into a big, satisfying dish. In fact, when you toss a bowl of zucchini or butternut squash noodles with a creamy basil pesto, you'll be getting your daily recommended amount of vegetables while feeling you're eating a decadent bowl of spaghetti. For example, a woman in her 40s should consume 2½ cups of vegetables per day. With just one bowl of zucchini noodles, she has achieved that— without having to force down a green juice or some steamed broccoli.

In short, spiralized vegetables can be "disguised" as pasta, noodles, and rice, transforming them into popular forms. Some unexpected guises include:

IN A FRITTATA (Chorizo and Avocado Zucchini Frittata, page 36)

IN A SOUP (Chicken Carrot Noodle Soup, page 76)

IN NACHOS (Spicy Butternut Squash Nachos, page 60)

IN SUSHI (Beet Rice Nori Rolls, page 106)

IN A DESSERT (Pecan and Carrot Almond Butter Bars, page 194)

These are just a few of the many creative capabilities and versatilities of spiralized vegetables—in fact, this book is full of them! You'll quickly find what works best for you.

Family and Kid-Friendly Cooking

So many parents complain, "I can't get my kids to eat vegetables!" Well, what child doesn't love spaghetti? Whether eating it messily with their hands at age 1 or with a fork at age 4, most kids love noodles. Make a simple bowl of zucchini noodles with tomato sauce and watch your toddler dig in—he or she will never know it's the "icky" green stuff. If spaghetti doesn't do the trick, you can make elbow macaroni carrot noodles and top them with a light cheese sauce (see page 131). When you master the spiralized bun (see page 26), you'll be able to create sandwiches out of heart-healthy veggies such as sweet potatoes. For an after-school snack, fit in a fruit-and-vegetable double whammy with the Apple-Potato Cheese Bun (page 119). You can also nurse your kid back to health with Chicken Carrot Noodle Soup (page 76) using carrots instead of pasta, thereby providing beta-carotene, a powerful phytonutrient that boosts the immune system's production of infection-fighting natural cells. But that'll be our little secret.

Even better, toddlers and young kids love to get in on spiralizing. Who wouldn't have fun seeing a vegetable magically turn into noodles? There's no better way to teach your children healthy eating habits than to have them help you in the kitchen. Inadvertently, your children will learn that vegetables are fun.

Spiralized cooking is family-friendly because it's fast. When you're juggling soccer practices, dance recitals, homework, and more, you don't have much time left for cooking nutritious meals. But it takes only about 30 seconds to spiralize a zucchini and only 2 to 3 minutes to cook the noodles to al dente (versus 5 minutes to boil water and 10 to 15 minutes to cook wheat pasta). To really save time, you can spiralize your vegetable noodles ahead. For information on preparing vegetable noodles in advance, see the tips on pages 28–29.

READY, SET, SPIRALIZE!

So, how does it work, exactly? Let's get into everything you need to know to start spiralizing in your own kitchen.

The What

One of the best things about spiralizing is that it introduces you to new vegetables. Eventually, you'll be in the grocery store asking yourself, "Can I spiralize that?" Maybe you'll find something you've never tasted before—or even something you hadn't heard of yet. With these guidelines, you'll know right away.

The vegetable or fruit must be solid, with no tough pit, seedy interior, or hollow core. The only exception here is butternut squash, whose bulbous bottom has a seedy center. Prior to spiralizing, just chop that part off—the rest of the vegetable fits the bill.

The vegetable must be at least 1½ inches in diameter for optimal spiralizing. If the vegetable is any smaller, it will be tough to get perfect pasta-like spirals; instead, you'll have half-moon shapes. The larger the diameter, the better.

The vegetable or fruit must be at least 1½ inches in length. While the vegetable won't yield many noodles this long, that's the shortest length you should use; otherwise, the vegetable will be mostly wasted.

The vegetable or fruit cannot be soft or juicy inside. The outer skin should be tough, unless you're peeling it. If you are peeling the skin, then the interior should be dense and firm. If you try spiralizing a juicy pineapple, for example, the fruit will fall apart.

There is one major exception to all these rules: eggplant. Because of its soft flesh and tiny seeds, it won't work well. When you load the eggplant in, you'll notice immediately upon cranking the handle that it resists the movement. Its flesh will be chopped, and any noodles that do materialize will be soft and break with a firm pinch. A very large eggplant yields only about 1½ cups of noodles—a big waste. I don't recommend spiralizing eggplant, and I have not included it in this cookbook.

So what *does* work? Depending on which part of the world you live in, you'll find some fruits or veggies unavailable locally or you will have some that other parts of the country do not have. If you don't see a familiar vegetable or fruit on the following list, refer to the above guidelines to determine if it can be spiralized.

These are my favorite vegetables for spiralizing, and they are the basis for recipes in this book:

Apple	Onion
Beet	Parsnip
Broccoli (stems only)	Pear
Butternut squash	Plantain
Cabbage	Radish
Carrot	Rutabaga
Celeriac (celery root)	Summer squash
Chayote	Sweet potato (and
Cucumber	yam)
Jícama	Turnip
Kohlrabi	White potato
	Zucchini

When choosing a vegetable or fruit, consider its texture, color, nutritional balance, and of course, flavor. For information regarding best uses, preparations, cooking methods, serving sizes, nutritional values, and health benefits of each specific vegetable and fruit on this list, see pages 208–217.

The How

We know *why* incorporating spiralized vegetables into our diets is beneficial, and we know *what* we can and cannot spiralize . . . but how do we actually *do* it?

Prepping

Prior to spiralizing, you must always prepare your vegetable or fruit. If the skin of whatever you are using is inedible, or if you prefer not to eat it, peel it off. However, do keep in mind that many important vitamins and nutrients in vegetables and fruits are found in the skin.

Next, be sure the ends of the fruit or vegetable are as even and flat as possible. If they are not flat (say, rounded, as for a beet), you can just slice off a small piece to flatten the ends.

If you are finding that a particular vegetable does not spiralize easily, it could be because there is not enough surface area for the spiralizer to grip on to. Remember, you're looking for a minimum of 1½ inches in diameter. Also, in an effort to get the vegetable as straight as possible and with flat ends, you may need to trim off edible parts of the vegetable or fruit; that can be frustrating, but save those trimmings for future cooking, or just snack along the way!

You also may want to cut some long vegetables in half crosswise to give yourself better leverage with the spiralizer. Generally, anything longer than 6 inches should be halved. This rule almost always applies to butternut squash, but also to some bigger sweet potatoes, zucchini, and cucumbers.

Choosing Your Blade

When you've prepped your vegetable, it's ready to be spiralized. You select the blade depending on what recipe you're making and what type of noodles it requires. Most spiralizers on the market today come with three or four blades. The recipes in this book indicate whether to use the A, B, C, or D blade. Here are descriptions to help you figure out which blades I'm indicating:

BLADE A: Yields thin, ribboned noodles similar to pappardelle.

BLADE B: Yields noodles similar to fettuccine.

BLADE C: Yields noodles similar to linguine and spaghetti.

BLADE D: Yields the thinnest noodles, similar to angel hair. (This blade should be used on skinnier vegetables. It can also be used interchangeably with blade C.)

BLADE A

BLADE B

BLADE C

My tool, the Inspiralizer, uses these lettered labels on the blade-changing knobs, but if yours is another brand, you'll want to check its manual so you know which blade makes which noodle. Most blades have either comb-like teeth or triangle-shaped spokes. The smaller the distance between the teeth or the smaller the triangular spokes, the thinner the noodle produced. If the blade doesn't have *any* teeth or triangular spokes, then it's always blade A.

If you don't have a spiralizer yet, you can still make spaghetti-like strands using a julienne peeler or mandolin. These won't yield long, spiral-like noodles, but they are a great way to start enjoying vegetable pasta!

Cooking with Spiralized Rice

	YIELDS (CUPS)	RAW OR COOKED	COOK TIME (MINUTES)
Beets	2	Both	10
Butternut squash	Up to 4	Cooked	10–15
Carrots	1½	Raw	5–10
Celeriac	Up to 4	Both	10–15
Jícama*	Up to 4	Both	5–10
Daikon radish*	2	Both	5–10
Kohlrabi	2	Both	5–10
Plantains	1	Cooked	10–15
Rutabaga	Up to 4	Cooked	10–15
Sweet potatoes	2	Cooked	10-–5
Turnips*	1½	Both	10
Zucchini	1½–2	Both	2–3

*Squeeze out excess moisture after pulsing and prior to cooking.

Beyond the Noodle

When you start spiralizing, you'll most likely begin by making pasta dishes. You'll rejoice in the fact that you're appreciating vegetables in a whole new way—as the superhero, not as the trusty sidekick. But after a while, you will wonder, "Okay, what's next?" The sky's the limit: you can Inspiralize any meal. It's always fun and is always surprising.

Spiralized Rice

One afternoon I was testing some new cooking methods, and I placed butternut squash noodles into boiling water. Big mistake; the noodles broke apart, practically disintegrating. It was a seemingly failed experiment, until I suddenly realized: it looked just like rice! I ran with it, making Spanish rice with ham and olives, sweet potato fried rice, risotto with peas, and even plantain rice and beans. I quickly realized this technique was just as powerful as making vegetable noodles.

With vegetable rice, you don't need expensive rice cookers, watery boil-in-a-bag grains, or mushy and preservative-laden frozen versions. Instead, in under 5 minutes, you can have a totally unprocessed and nutritious option. This party trick makes it possible to reinvent more of your favorites, typically those indulgent dishes. Burrito bowls, stuffed peppers, risottos, pilafs, casseroles, curries, and paella—you name it. You can make vegetable rice from all vegetables that can be spiralized, except those that have a high water content. The chart opposite shows which vegetables make the best rice, how much they yield, and how to cook them.

There are many ways to cook spiralized rice:

BAKED IN THE OVEN: Vegetable rice works well in casseroles. It can be added raw and then slowly baked until cooked through.

SAUTÉED IN A SKILLET: Cook the vegetable rice with your oil of choice, tossing occasionally, and season to your preference.

SIMMERED IN A BROTH OR SAUCE: Add the vegetable rice to a simmering sauce or pour broth over the rice and simmer until cooked.

How to Make Spiralized Rice

Spiralize the vegetable of choice using blade C or blade D. Place the noodles in a food processor and pulse until they look rice-like. For those vegetables that need draining, just squeeze the rice over the sink to rid it of excess moisture before cooking.

Spiralized Buns

My idea for spiralized buns originated during the ramen burger craze in the summer of 2013, in Williamsburg, Brooklyn. At Smorgasburg, an outdoor pop-up food market, hundreds of people were waiting in line for ramen burgers. They are exactly what they sound like: a burger on a bun made from packed ramen noodles. Seeing them, I immediately wanted to create a healthier version—so I did! (See below.)

Vegetable noodle buns are not only gluten free but also full of nutrients, unlike the typical puffy wheat or potato bun. These buns can be used to sandwich burgers, serve as open-faced sandwiches, or even be the basis for miniature pizzas. Check the chart on this page to see which vegetables are best for use as buns and how many buns can be made with each.

	YIELDS (BUNS)
Large potatoes (all types)	2–3
Large parsnips	1–2
Large rutabaga	6
Large celeriac	3–4
Large plantain	1–2

Let's Get Cooking

I'm not a professionally trained chef, nor have I ever worked in a restaurant kitchen. I have definitely roasted meats too long and whisked eggs backward, and I can't effortlessly mince garlic. But that's okay. On the whole, there's no right or wrong way to cook. For those of us who love to cook but don't have the means or desire to acquire culinary training,

How to Make Spiralized Buns

Spiralize your vegetable of choice using blade C. Season and sauté the noodles in a large skillet. Transfer to a medium bowl, add an egg, and toss to coat. Pack into a ramekin or similar vessel and place foil or wax paper directly onto the noodles. Press down with your hands or a weighted can, then allow to set for 15 minutes in the refrigerator. Heat 1 tablespoon olive oil in a large skillet over medium heat. When the oil is shimmering, invert the molded noodle cake into the pan. Sear until the bun is firm and browned on both sides, about 5 minutes.

trial-and-error learning can go a long way. With spiralizing, you really enjoy being in the kitchen because not only is the spiralizing fun and easy, but you're also healthfully transforming your meals in a stunning way!

For a few years now, I've been spiralizing nearly every day, multiple times a day. I've tried to spiralize every conceivable vegetable and fruit, and I've had my share of "oops" and "aha!" moments. With my tips and tricks, you'll have all the information and forewarnings you need for a seamless experience.

Clean the Spiralizer Regularly

Certain vegetables (beets, carrots, sweet potatoes) are brightly colored and have oils and juices that can easily stain your spiralizer if you're not careful. I suggest buying a round palm brush solely for cleaning the spiralizer. The brush will make it easier to scrub the blades and remove any discoloration before it sets. Use soap and water, and clean just as soon as you finish spiralizing. The blades can be sharp, so the dedicated brush will save you from ruining others.

Avoid a Watery Sauce with Zucchini Noodles

The number one e-mail question I get from my readers is, "Why are my zucchini noodles sitting in a pool of liquid?" If you're using a tomato-based sauce, the chances are there will be excess liquid in your pasta bowl. The longer the zucchini noodles sit in a sauce like this, the more time they have to release their natural moisture, making the whole dish runny. Well, this is to be expected, since zucchini are 95 percent water! What's the silver lining? Foods rich in water cleanse your body naturally by providing up to a liter of fluid daily. Since most vegetables are high in fiber and water, they digest more quickly than other foods, allowing the body to use its energy for detoxifying instead of digesting.

Nevertheless, you can reduce the amount of water that will result. Here are some key tricks:

A 70:30 NOODLE-TO-SAUCE RATIO. Lean heavier on the noodles—add more noodles or simply use less sauce.

PAT THE VEGETABLES VERY DRY BEFORE COOKING. This is especially important for cucumber noodles. Patting dry with paper towels or a kitchen cloth towel will remove excess moisture that appears when the inside of the vegetable is exposed after spiralizing.

FULLY REDUCE YOUR SAUCE BEFORE ADDING TO YOUR VEGGIE NOODLES. Simmer your sauce until it's thick so there is no excess liquid. Doing so also concentrates the flavors.

ADD FOODS TO YOUR DISH THAT WILL SOAK UP MOISTURE. Stir in beans, cheeses, meats, and whole wheat bread crumbs. They all absorb liquid, thereby thickening your sauce.

COOK THE NOODLES SEPARATELY AND DRAIN THEM BEFORE ADDING THE SAUCE. If you are not in a rush, and don't mind dirtying extra dishes, cook the noodles briefly with only a little cooking spray in a heated skillet; allow to drain in a colander, and pat dry. When your sauce is done, pour it over the cooked noodles and then serve.

USE PASTA TONGS TO DRAIN THE NOODLES WHEN SERVING. Never pour out the contents of your skillet into a bowl to serve. When your pasta is cooked and ready to serve, remove the noodles with pasta tongs, allowing any excess moisture to drip off or remain in the pan.

Cutting the Noodles with Scissors

If you could continuously spiralize a vegetable with no breaks, it would yield one ridiculously long noodle. A reader once sent me a video of her kid jump roping with a zucchini noodle! Long noodles from perfectly straight and uniform vegetables are tough to serve and portion out. To make serving easier, use kitchen scissors to trim the noodles after spiralizing. You can go inch by inch or just grab a bunch and roughly snip. Either way, you'll get shorter noodles that are easier to divide onto plates and easier to eat. If you forget this step, don't worry, though—you can still do it after they've cooked.

Avoid Half-Moon Noodles

You will notice that the spiralizer slices some of the vegetable into half-moon shapes while you're making the spiral noodles. This happens mostly when the vegetable moves off center. To avoid this, simply stop and reposition your vegetable or fruit so that it keeps centered on the cylindrical coring blade. With smaller vegetables, you may have to do this repeatedly. Also, be sure the ends of your vegetables are flat. Uneven ends are tough to secure in the spiralizer and will cause the vegetable to dislodge or misalign.

If you end up with a heaping pile of half-moons, don't throw them out. Use them in a pasta salad; their little shape takes nicely to salad dressing and resembles big elbow macaroni pasta.

Store Your Spiralized Veggies in the Refrigerator or Freezer for Plan-Ahead Meals

Adopting a healthier diet requires staying focused and avoiding temptations. Meal planning, therefore, becomes your best friend. Nothing's worse than looking in your refrigerator and finding only condiments. When that happens, you are inclined to order a pizza or get "the usual" at your favorite takeout place.

To avoid such situations, you can store prepared vegetable noodles and vegetable rices in your refrigerator. *All* vegetable noodles can be prepared in advance and refrigerated or frozen for future use. Just line a glass or plastic container with paper towels and seal in an airtight container.

All vegetable noodles store in the refrigerator for up to 4 days. After 4 or 5 days, though, they will stiffen and lose their flavor. The following are exceptions to this rule:

CUCUMBERS last only 2 or 3 days in the refrigerator because of their very high water content.

APPLES, PEARS, AND WHITE POTATOES brown (oxidize) when spiralized, and are thereafter difficult to prep in advance.

Vegetable noodles that freeze well include sweet potatoes, rutabaga, carrots, beets, butternut squash, parsnips, celeriac, kohlrabi, and broccoli stems. As they defrost, they will wilt, making them even easier to cook.

You can also save whole leftover spiralized meals in the refrigerator for a few days. Be aware that if you are using zucchini or cucumber noodles, though, excess moisture will slowly be released the longer the leftovers sit in the fridge. When reheating, drain away some liquid first to avoid a soupy sauce. This isn't a problem with other vegetable noodles.

The Inspiralized Kitchen

Certain kitchen tools are helpful for easily whipping up the meals in this book. In order of importance, consider having on hand:

FOOD PROCESSOR: Food processors are not only necessary for making spiralized rice but also are helpful for making clean salad dressings, pasta sauces, and bread crumbs. No need to buy a giant one that won't fit in your kitchen; I use a 3-cup food processor and that size works well.

PASTA TONGS: To properly cook your vegetable noodles, you need tongs to toss them. This tool will also help you serve your finished recipes. I suggest a rubber pair for their gentleness when handling delicate vegetables.

QUALITY CHEF'S KNIFE: Before I started cooking, I never understood why professional chefs were so attached to their knives, but now I get it! Some vegetables are tough to peel and prep for spiralizing, such as celeriac, butternut squash, and rutabaga. Without a quality knife that can easily cut through the flesh, your cooking experience may be less than pleasant.

NONSTICK SKILLETS: All my recipes require nonstick skillets, for a simple reason: cooking vegetable pasta in a regular skillet can be disastrous—the noodles stick, rip, and fall apart. If you don't already have one, start with a large nonstick skillet, then add to your collection later. I recommend 8-, 10-, and 12-inch skillets.

VEGETABLE PEELER: Carrots, beets, butternut squash, jícama, rutabaga, kohlrabi, celeriac, and plantain must be peeled prior to spiralizing. Other vegetables, such as zucchini, can be peeled for a softer noodle, but doing so is not necessary. Peeling with a knife can be inefficient, difficult, dangerous, and time-consuming. I use two peelers—one with ridges for the very tough-skinned vegetables and one without for softer skins, like zucchini.

ROUND PALM BRUSH: A dedicated brush for cleaning your spiralizer. Refer to page 27 for more details.

Other essential kitchen tools include a spatula, a cutting board, and at least two baking sheets. And some other tools that would be helpful, but not completely necessary, are a high-speed blender, a slow cooker, and a grill pan.

The Inspiralized Pantry

Stocking your pantry with interesting condiments, seasonings, and foods will keep you from becoming overwhelmed by grocery shopping, whether you're spiralizing or not. Many of the following ingredients appear repeatedly in this cookbook because they are easy, inexpensive ways to add a ton of flavor to a meal without extra calories, carbohydrates, or fat. With these items on hand, you'll always be able to create a nutritious meal.

EXTRA-VIRGIN OLIVE OIL: A heart-healthy fat, olive oil is great in everything from salad dressing to stir-fries. Most of my recipes begin with a tablespoon of olive oil, which helps fit in meeting your daily recommended serving of fat. Do keep in mind that olive oil is high in calories and should be used in moderation if you are on a weight-loss journey.

EXTRA-VIRGIN COCONUT OIL: Coconuts are super-rich in nutrients. As an oil, they add a light coconut taste and associated nutrients to your meals, which is great in Asian sauces. This oil is high in calories and should be used in moderation if you are concerned about weight loss.

ASSORTED CANNED BEANS: I always keep my pantry stocked with cannellini beans, chickpeas, black beans, and pinto beans. They're a quick and easy protein source to add to any dish.

LOW-SODIUM CHICKEN, BEEF, AND VEGETABLE BROTH: Broth is a healthy way to add flavor to any vegetable noodle dish.

SESAME OIL: Toasted sesame oil is ideal for flavoring Asian dressings, stir-fries, and soups.

NUTS AND SEEDS: These both give the benefit of healthy fats and proteins. Add them to pastas, salads, and rices. I love sprinkling crushed pistachios over zucchini pasta or adding pepitas to a pasta with black beans and avocado for a Mexican flair. Almonds, walnuts, cashews, peanuts, macadamia nuts, and Brazil nuts are all great choices!

CHUNK LIGHT TUNA (IN WATER): This type of tuna has the least amount of mercury. Packed in water, it also won't add unnecessary calories and fat from oil. Plus, it's a lean protein source that is ready to eat without cooking!

LOW-SODIUM SOY SAUCE: Soy sauce pairs well with sesame oil to make a quick Asian-inspired dish with lots of flavor for just a little prep time. Soy sauce is very high in sodium, though, so be sure to get the low-sodium kind.

RED WINE VINEGAR: Red wine vinegar is the ultimate ingredient for creating light salad dressings, thanks to its tangy, fresh taste and low-calorie value.

BALSAMIC VINEGAR: Blame the Italian in me, but I think balsamic vinegar is the best! It makes an easy, tasty marinade that's low in calories and can be whisked into dressings to lend a tart kick.

APPLE CIDER VINEGAR: Made from apples instead of grapes, cider vinegar can be used in place of red wine vinegar or balsamic vinegar in dressings and marinades. It has incredible detoxifying and pH-balancing capabilities. Its sweeter taste is nice in raw salads, such as the Beet Superfood Bowl (page 140).

SPICES: I always cook with dried spices because they add flavor *and* nutrients. My favorites are chili powder, oregano, smoked paprika, ground cumin, garlic powder, and red pepper flakes.

SEA SALT AND PEPPERCORNS: These standard pantry items have a greater punch when freshly ground. If you want to make one great change to your kitchen pantry (and if you're not doing this already), it would be to throw away your salt and pepper shakers and replace them with grinders. Sea salt and peppercorns are less processed than the standards and are more flavorful. You'll wonder how you cooked without them!

JARRED PASTA SAUCES: My grandparents might be horrified, but I always have cans of my favorite tomato-basil pasta sauce in my pantry for last-minute meals. Just be sure the ingredient list has whole tomatoes (and no sugar, no dairy, and preferably no added salt).

CANNED DICED TOMATOES: When it's not summertime, tasty fresh tomatoes are hard to come by, so diced canned tomatoes tend to be preferable. Look for a no-salt-added variety.

OLIVE OIL COOKING SPRAY: Cooking spray is essential for coating baking sheets and it also works well for lightly sautéing vegetable noodles.

How to Use This Book

As you've realized, vegetable pasta is not only nutritious and filling but it's also easy to make. Spiralizing is for all ages, diet lifestyles, and cooking skill levels. Even a college student in a dorm can make a big bowl of pasta using a spiralizer and the microwave!

I—a woman with an appetite for good food and a mind for healthy living—wrote all the recipes in this cookbook. They are easy to make and include ingredients that you can find in your local grocery store. Nothing is intended to be daunting or complicated. The inspiration for most of my recipes came from classic Italian pasta dishes that my grandparents cooked or food I tasted when dining out.

In an effort to present dishes that are truly healthy, you will not find the following ingredients in any of my recipes:

Butter	Mayonnaise
Dairy milk	Cream cheese
Cream	White breads
Sugar	

Can you make your fettuccini with whipping cream and your tomato cream sauce with butter? Of course, and it will be delicious. This cookbook is not just an alternative to wheat pasta; it is also a clean-eating cookbook with healthy sauces, lean meats, and moderate amounts of fats and carbohydrates. With this cookbook, you will be *Inspiralizing* whole meals, not just "cooking" them! Experiment with these recipes; if you prefer the indulgent stuff, go ahead. Remember that part of healthy eating is moderation.

While I refrain from using most dairy products in my recipes, I do eat some. Healthy living is all about what works for your own personal style. Cheese is an integral part of my family's culture and it's my biggest passion in cooking. I had to draw the line somewhere along my healthy journey, and that meant using cheese but only in moderation.

Recipe Features

Each recipe includes symbol indicators to give you a quick overview of its difficulty rating and nutritional information. First, the number of spirals is a measure of how difficult the recipe is to make:

- ∽ **ONE SPIRAL:** Very easy, not much cooking required, basic spiralizing

- ∽∽ **TWO SPIRALS:** Medium difficulty, more cooking required

- ∽∽∽ **THREE SPIRALS:** Most difficult, many steps required, more handling of the spiralized vegetables

However, don't let a three-spiral recipe intimidate you; it mostly just means that the recipe will take you a bit more time on account of the extra steps involved.

The spiralized ingredient in each recipe list follows this format:

1 medium zucchini, spiralized with BLADE A

The vegetable should be spiralized *prior* to beginning the recipe, along with doing any other ingredient preparations, such as chopping, mincing, and dicing. The ingredients are listed in the order in which they are used in the recipe. Whichever blade is specified is the one you should use to spiralize the vegetable. (See page 23 for a reminder of which blade does what.)

You'll also see some recipes classified as gluten free, paleo, vegan, or vegetarian.

(V) **VEGAN:** Does not contain any animal products

(VT) **VEGETARIAN:** Meat, poultry, and fowl-free, but may contain dairy and/or eggs

(GF) **GLUTEN-FREE:** Does not contain any gluten

(P) **PALEO:** Excludes dairy, grain products, and any processed food

And finally, all recipes include the following nutritional information: calories, fat, carbohydrates, sodium, protein, and sugar for the stated portion size. This nutritional information was calculated primarily using data from the USDA National Nutrient Database for Standard Reference.

Now, are you excited to eat? Grab your spiralizer and join me as we revolutionize the way we regard vegetables. We're going to have fun, whittle down our waistlines, and tantalize and surprise our taste buds. This book was written with passion, love, and commitment to living a lifestyle that satisfies the tummy and supports a healthy heart and mind. What would I call that lifestyle? *Inspiralized.*

BREAKFASTS

Chorizo and Avocado Zucchini Frittata
with Manchego–Pea Shoot Salad

Pesto Sun-dried Tomato Egg Muffins

Blueberry Sweet Potato Waffles

Ham and Rutabaga Breakfast Skillet

Cinnamon-Walnut Protein Muffins

Huevos Rancheros

"Everything Bagel" Breakfast Buns

Savoy Cabbage Breakfast Burrito

Kohlrabi and Sausage Breakfast Sauté
with Spicy Salsa Verde

Chorizo and Avocado Zucchini Frittata with Manchego–Pea Shoot Salad

MAKES
4 servings

GF

TIME TO PREPARE
20 minutes

TIME TO COOK
25 minutes

NUTRITIONAL INFORMATION
SERVING SIZE: ¼ frittata +
1 packed cup salad
Calories: 451
Fat: 32 g
Carbohydrates: 24 g
Sodium: 417 mg
Protein: 48 g
Sugar: 11 g

ALSO WORKS WITH
Kohlrabi · Potatoes ·
Parsnips · Beets ·
Chayote

If you've never put leftover pasta into a frittata, now's your time to try it—but with zucchini noodles. These noodles add texture, heartiness, and nutrients. The mild cheese and dainty yet tangy pea shoots are perfect accompaniments for this spicy and rich frittata. I like to make the frittata as "breakfast for dinner," but it will certainly wow any guests for brunch, with the spirals of zucchini peeking through the baked eggs.

For the frittata
Cooking spray

2 spicy chorizo links, casings removed, meat crumbled

1 avocado, cubed

1 large garlic clove, minced

2 medium zucchini, spiralized with BLADE C

3 large eggs plus 9 egg whites, lightly beaten

Salt and pepper

For the salad
2 tablespoons lemon juice

3 tablespoons olive oil

2 tablespoons sherry vinegar

2 teaspoons honey
Salt and pepper

6 cups diced pea shoots

¼ cup diced manchego cheese

If you can't find pea shoots for the salad, use watercress instead.

1 Make the frittata. Preheat the oven to 375 degrees. Coat a large skillet with cooking spray and place over medium heat. When water flicked onto the skillet sizzles, add the chorizo, avocado, and garlic and cook for 5 minutes or until the chorizo crumbles begin to brown. Add the zucchini noodles and toss to combine. Spread the ingredients in an even layer.

2 Pour the eggs over the noodles and season to taste with salt and pepper. Cook for 2 minutes or until the eggs are set on the bottom, then transfer the skillet to the oven and bake for about 15 minutes or until the eggs have completely set and begin to brown on the edges.

3 Make the salad. Whisk together the lemon juice, olive oil, sherry, honey, and salt and pepper in a small bowl. Toss with the pea shoots and manchego.

4 Slice the frittata into 4 or 8 pieces. Serve with the pea shoot salad.

Pesto Sun-Dried Tomato Egg Muffins

MAKES
6 muffins

GF

VT

TIME TO PREPARE
15 minutes

TIME TO COOK
25 minutes

NUTRITIONAL INFORMATION
SERVING SIZE: **1 muffin + 1 heaping tablespoon pesto**
Calories: 303
Fat: 24 g
Carbohydrates: 13 g
Sodium: 94 mg
Protein: 11 g
Sugar: 1 g

ALSO WORKS WELL WITH
Zucchini

Usually when I make the trip to my parents' home in New Jersey for a birthday or similar celebration, my mother serves brunch. From the serving pieces to the toothpicks in the appetizer spread, she always makes these occasions special. She once prepared the most adorable egg muffins, which inspired this recipe. They take the presentation up a notch—the potato noodles are visible from the outside, which is a conversation starter. They are also a complete meal, with your protein, starch, and vegetables all in one!

1 Preheat the oven to 375 degrees.

2 Make the pesto. Combine the ingredients in a food processor and puree to a thick paste, periodically scraping down the sides. Transfer to a container and keep covered so the pesto does not brown.

3 Make the muffins. Heat the olive oil in a large nonstick skillet over medium heat. When the oil is shimmering, add the potato noodles and season with the garlic powder, salt, and pepper. Cover and cook for 6 to 8 minutes, tossing occasionally, until the noodles wilt and begin to brown. When the noodles are cooked through, remove from the skillet and set aside. Using the same skillet, again over medium heat, add the spinach and cook until wilted, a minute or two.

For the pesto
- 3 cups packed fresh basil leaves
- ¼ cup pine nuts
- ¼ cup olive oil
- Salt and pepper
- 1 large garlic clove, minced

For the muffins
- 1 tablespoon olive oil
- 1 large Yukon Gold potato, peeled, spiralized with BLADE C
- 1 teaspoon garlic powder
- Salt and pepper
- 3 cups packed fresh baby spinach
- Olive oil or cooking spray
- 7 large eggs, lightly beaten
- ⅓ cup plus 2 teaspoons finely chopped sun-dried tomatoes

4 Coat a 6-cup nonstick muffin tin with cooking spray or olive oil. To each cup, add ½ inch of beaten egg. Then add about 1 inch of the potato noodles. Top each with a few leaves of wilted spinach and 3 teaspoons of the sun-dried tomato. Slowly pour the remaining egg on top until the cups are full. Generously sprinkle the tops with more pepper.

5 Bake for 15 minutes or until the eggs are set. Remove from the oven, allow to cool in the muffin tin for 1 minute, then carefully remove the muffins and serve, each drizzled with a bit of pesto.

~~~~~~~~~~~~~~~~~~~~~~~~~

For a quicker-to-make and lighter muffin, use zucchini noodles instead of potato. The zucchini doesn't need to be seasoned or cooked beforehand; it simply adds a nice crunch to the muffin.

~~~~~~~~~~~~~~~~~~~~~~~~~

Blueberry Sweet Potato Waffles

MAKES
2 waffles

GF

VT

P

TIME TO PREPARE
15 minutes

TIME TO COOK
10 minutes

NUTRITIONAL INFORMATION
SERVING SIZE: **1 waffle +
½ tablespoon pure
maple syrup**
Calories: 150
Fat: 3 g
Carbohydrates: 28 g
Sodium: 70 mg
Protein: 4 g
Sugar: 13 g

These waffles are as clean eating as it gets. When you take your first bite, you will taste the plump blueberries, spicy cinnamon, and soft sweet potato. Instead of using flour, sugar, and butter—or, worse, something frozen in a box—try this recipe. While they don't have the fluffiness of traditional waffles, they do offer an interesting texture, and the natural sugar in the sweet potatoes gives them a special sweetness. With warmed blueberries and maple syrup to accompany, these waffles are sure to become a brunch favorite.

1 Preheat a waffle iron. Place the sweet potato noodles in a bowl and toss with the cinnamon. Place a large skillet over medium heat and coat with cooking spray. When water flicked onto the skillet sizzles, add the seasoned sweet potato noodles and cover. Cook for 5 to 7 minutes or until the noodles have completely softened.

2 Transfer the noodles to a large bowl and add the egg, vanilla, and blueberries. Toss gently to combine until the noodles are coated, taking care not to break them.

3 Coat the waffle iron with cooking spray and carefully pour in half of the noodle mixture, taking care to fill all the cavities with noodles. Cook the waffle following the manufacturer's instructions. When the waffle is done, transfer to a plate and keep warm while you make the second waffle. Drizzle a bit of maple syrup over each and serve.

1 medium sweet potato, peeled,
   spiralized with BLADE C
1 teaspoon ground cinnamon
   Cooking spray
1 medium egg, lightly beaten
½ teaspoon vanilla extract
½ cup fresh blueberries
1 tablespoon maple syrup or to taste

Add dairy-free chocolate chips for extra sweetness.

Ham and Rutabaga Breakfast Skillet

MAKES
4 to 6 servings

GF

P

TIME TO PREPARE
10 minutes

TIME TO COOK
35 minutes

NUTRITIONAL INFORMATION
SERVING SIZE: **1 heaping cup (1 egg)**
Calories: 171
Fat: 8 g
Carbohydrates: 10 g
Sodium: 658 mg
Protein: 14 g
Sugar: 7 g

ALSO WORKS WELL WITH
Sweet Potatoes

You might not typically eat rice for breakfast, but when it's this spiralized rice, you'll welcome the change in routine. Starting off your morning with a hefty serving of vegetables ensures a productive and focused day. The eggs bake nestled in the rutabaga-rice mixture and, when broken to serve, coat the rice and ham with a warm, yolky sauce. Every bite is slightly sweet and comforting.

1 Preheat the oven to 400 degrees. Heat the olive oil in a large nonstick skillet over medium heat. Add the garlic, onion, and red pepper flakes. Cook for 2 minutes or until the onion is translucent. Add the rutabaga rice, ham, kale, paprika, cumin, and tomatoes. Stir to combine well and season with salt and pepper. Add the broth and cook for 2 to 3 minutes more, or until reduced somewhat, stirring occasionally.

2 Create four evenly spaced cavities in the mixture and crack an egg into each. Transfer to the oven and bake for about 10 minutes or until the eggs are set.

3 Serve hot family style, sprinkled with parsley.

1 tablespoon olive oil

2 large garlic cloves, minced

1 cup diced white onion

Pinch of red pepper flakes

1 small rutabaga, peeled, spiralized with BLADE C, then riced (see page 25)

1 cup cubed ham

1½ packed cups chopped fresh kale

1 teaspoon smoked paprika

1 teaspoon ground cumin

1 cup chopped ripe tomatoes, with juices

Salt and pepper

½ cup low-sodium chicken broth

4 large eggs

1 tablespoon chopped fresh parsley

Cinnamon-Walnut Protein Muffins

MAKES
4 large muffins

GF

TIME TO PREPARE
10 minutes

VT

TIME TO COOK
25 minutes

P

NUTRITIONAL INFORMATION
SERVING SIZE: **1 muffin**
Calories: 130
Fat: 6 g
Carbohydrates: 17 g
Sodium: 114 mg
Protein: 4 g
Sugar: 9 g

I hadn't used protein powder until I started drinking smoothies for breakfast. One day I added some and I just never stopped—it kept me feeling full for much longer. Now, I even add protein powder to baked goods. Keep yourself nourished and satisfied all morning with these flavorful and sweet muffins.

1 Preheat the oven to 375 degrees. Combine the sweet potato rice, cinnamon, protein powder, and baking soda in a medium bowl. Add the egg, honey, and vanilla, and mix thoroughly. Stir in the raisins and walnuts and mix again.

2 Coat a large-cup muffin tin lightly with cooking spray. Spoon the batter evenly into each cup and bake for 23 to 25 minutes or until a toothpick skewer in the center comes out clean. Remove from the oven and let the tin sit for a minute or two, then invert to remove the muffins. Allow to cool for 5 minutes before eating.

1 medium sweet potato, peeled, spiralized with BLADE C, then riced (see page 25)

¼ teaspoon ground cinnamon

1 tablespoon protein powder

¼ teaspoon baking soda

1 large egg

1 tablespoon honey

¼ teaspoon vanilla extract

2 tablespoons raisins

¼ cup chopped walnuts

Cooking spray

If you use a vanilla-flavored protein powder, skip the vanilla extract here. I prefer plant-based protein powders, such as those derived from peas or brown rice.

Huevos Rancheros

MAKES
2 servings

GF

VT

TIME TO PREPARE
20 minutes

TIME TO COOK
25 minutes

NUTRITIONAL INFORMATION
SERVING SIZE: **1 plantain tortilla with sauce + 1 egg and toppings**
Calories: 623
Fat: 32 g
Carbohydrates: 69 g
Sodium: 376 mg
Protein: 22 g
Sugar: 23 g

Huevos rancheros are Lu's go-to meal when we're out for brunch. At this point, I think he can tell you which restaurants in New York City, Hoboken, and Jersey City have the best versions of this classic Mexican breakfast dish. The plantain rice tortilla serves as the fried tortilla, and it's both more flavorful and lower in saturated fat than the usual. As my official taste tester and huevos rancheros expert, Lu approves of this recipe and I know you will, too.

For the tortillas and roasted corn
Cooking spray
1 medium-ripe plantain, peeled, spiralized with BLADE C, then riced (see page 25)
1 large egg
1 tablespoon coconut flakes
Salt and pepper
1 ear of corn, husk and silks removed
Chili powder

For the ranchero sauce
1 tablespoon olive oil
1 teaspoon minced garlic
½ cup diced white onion
1 teaspoon tomato paste
½ cup canned diced tomatoes, with juice
½ cup canned black beans, drained and rinsed

1 avocado, cubed
1 teaspoon chili powder
1 tablespoon finely chopped seeded jalapeño
1 tablespoon chopped fresh cilantro
1 teaspoon ground cumin
1 teaspoon dried Mexican seasoning or oregano
Salt and pepper

To finish the dish
¼ cup shredded Monterey Jack cheese
Cooking spray
2 large eggs

These huevos rancheros still taste incredible without the cheese, so if you're watching your waistline or are dairy-free, just skip the cheese.

(recipe continues)

1 Preheat the oven to 400 degrees.

2 Make the tortillas. Line one baking sheet with parchment paper and lightly coat a second sheet with cooking spray.

3 Place the plantain rice in a bowl and add the egg and coconut flakes. Stir to combine thoroughly and season with salt and pepper. Scoop out half of the mixture and place it on one side of the lined baking sheet. Using your hands, flatten the mixture and round the edges to make it like a tortilla. Repeat with the remaining mixture on the opposite end of the lined baking sheet.

4 Place the ear of corn on the coated baking sheet and generously season with salt, pepper, and chili powder. Transfer both baking sheets to the oven. Bake the plantain tortillas for 15 to 17 minutes or until they are firm and golden brown on top. Remove the corn when it's easily pierced with a fork, in 12 to 15 minutes.

5 Prepare the ranchero sauce. Heat the olive oil in a medium saucepan over medium-low heat. When the oil is shimmering, add the garlic. Cook for 30 seconds or until fragrant, then add the onion, tomato paste, and tomatoes. Cook for 2 to 3 minutes, until the tomato sauce begins to reduce. Add half the beans, the avocado, chili powder, jalapeño, cilantro, cumin, and Mexican seasoning. Season with salt and pepper. Reduce the heat and simmer for about 5 minutes or until sauce thickens to a creamy consistency.

6 While the sauce cooks, mash the remaining beans with a fork or potato masher.

7 Finish the dish. Transfer the plantain tortillas to a large oven-safe skillet. (If they both don't fit, use two small skillets.) Mix the mashed beans with the ranchero sauce and divide the mixture evenly between the tortillas, then top with the cheese and bake for 5 minutes or until the cheese melts.

8 Place a large nonstick skillet over medium heat and coat with cooking spray. When a bit of water flicked onto the skillet sizzles, crack in the 2 eggs and fry until the whites are set, about 3 minutes.

9 Transfer the tortillas to serving plates. Slice the corn kernels off the cob and divide most of the kernels evenly over the tortillas. Top each tortilla with a fried egg, then garnish with the remaining corn kernels and serve.

"Everything Bagel" Breakfast Buns

MAKES
4 buns

GF

TIME TO PREPARE
15 minutes

TIME TO COOK
25 minutes

NUTRITIONAL INFORMATION
SERVING SIZE: **1 bun**
Calories: 170
Fat: 9 g
Carbohydrates: 19 g
Sodium: 227 mg
Protein: 5 g
Sugar: 2 g

ALSO WORKS WELL WITH
Sweet Potatoes

If you ask most kids who grew up in Jersey what their favorite breakfast is, they'll most likely come back with "Taylor ham, egg, and cheese on a bagel." Taylor ham, or pork roll, is apparently indigenous to NJ—and I always had mine on an everything bagel. The mere scent of this doughy breakfast favorite makes me recall those wonderful mornings when my mother would bring home a fresh batch from the local shop. Of course, I had to Inspiralize the undeniably best type of bagel in the world.

1 Make the bagel mix. Combine the ingredients in a small bowl and set aside.

2 Make the buns. Heat a large nonstick skillet over medium heat and coat with cooking spray. When water flicked onto the skillet sizzles, add the potato noodles and season with salt and pepper. Cover and cook, tossing occasionally, for 5 to 7 minutes or until the potatoes are golden brown. Transfer to a large bowl and allow to cool for 2 minutes.

3 Stir in the eggs and bagel mix. Toss until the potato noodles are evenly coated. Fill four 6-ounce ramekins halfway with the potato noodles. Cover each with a piece of foil or wax paper, pressing it firmly down onto the potato noodles to compress them. Refrigerate for at least 15 minutes to set.

For the bagel mix
1 teaspoon poppy seeds
1 teaspoon sesame seeds
1¼ teaspoons garlic powder
1 teaspoon onion powder
½ teaspoon coarse sea salt
¼ teaspoon freshly cracked black peppercorns

For the buns
Cooking spray
1 large Idaho potato, peeled, spiralized with BLADE C
Salt and pepper
1 large egg and 1 egg white, lightly beaten
2 tablespoons olive oil

(recipe continues)

4 Heat 1 tablespoon of the olive oil in a large nonstick skillet over medium heat. When the oil is shimmering, add the buns two at a time, flipping each out of its ramekin into the skillet and patting the bottom until the bun falls out. Cook for 3 minutes or until set, being sure to push in any stray noodles. Carefully flip and cook another 2 to 3 minutes or until the buns are completely set and browned on both sides. Repeat with the other ramekins, adding the remaining tablespoon oil as needed.

5 Serve the bagel buns with the spreads and toppings of your choice.

If you don't have 6-ounce ramekins, you can still make this and other bun recipes. Just heat $\frac{1}{2}$ tablespoon olive oil in a skillet, and instead of packing the noodles into a ramekin and refrigerating, put $\frac{1}{2}$ cup of the mixture in the middle of the skillet. Immediately form it into a patty and flatten with a spatula, taking care to keep the noodles tightly packed. Flip the patty after about 2 minutes, or after the bottom sets, and cook for another 2 minutes, flattening again with the back of a spatula.

Savoy Cabbage Breakfast Burrito

MAKES
2 burritos

TIME TO PREPARE
10 minutes

TIME TO COOK
15 minutes

NUTRITIONAL INFORMATION
SERVING SIZE: 1 burrito
Calories: 420
Fat: 27 g
Carbohydrates: 24 g
Sodium: 584 mg
Protein: 22 g
Sugar: 5 g

ALSO WORKS WELL WITH
Rutabaga · Beets ·
Carrots · Parsnips

Nothing says breakfast like bacon, eggs, and potatoes. But how do you put a new twist on such basic ingredients? You spiralize them into a burrito! Burritos are great because they can be prepped in advance and are easily transported—you can wrap this bad boy in tinfoil and eat it on the road, at work, at a picnic, or wherever. The savoy cabbage works wonders here, keeping all the ingredients intact without breaking apart. Plus, you're getting your greens first thing in the morning. Top the burrito with Sriracha or ketchup for even more flavor.

1 In a small bowl, mash the avocado and season with salt and pepper. Spread half the avocado mixture in the center of each cabbage leaf.

2 Place a large nonstick skillet over medium heat. When a little water flicked onto the skillet sizzles, add the bacon. Cook until crisped to your liking, then set aside on a paper towel–lined plate to drain.

3 Discard half the fat from the pan and add the sweet potato noodles. Cover and cook over medium heat, tossing occasionally, for 5 to 8 minutes or until wilted. Divide the noodles evenly between the cabbage leaves, layering them over the avocado.

4 In the same skillet, still over medium heat, crack the eggs and scramble, cooking until set. Spread the eggs over the sweet potato noodles. Top each wrap with two pieces of bacon. Roll up like a burrito and serve.

1 avocado, cubed
  Salt and pepper
2 leaves of savoy cabbage
4 bacon slices
1 sweet potato, peeled, spiralized with
  BLADE C
4 large eggs, lightly beaten

If you'd like to turn this wrap into a more traditional rice-based burrito, place the sweet potato noodles into a food processor and pulse until rice-like. Then, toss them in a skillet with some coconut or extra-virgin olive oil and salt and pepper for 5 to 7 minutes or until cooked through. Add them to the mix and roll up like a burrito!

Kohlrabi and Sausage Breakfast Sauté with Spicy Salsa Verde

MAKES
2 servings

GF

P

TIME TO PREPARE
15 minutes

TIME TO COOK
10 minutes

NUTRITIONAL INFORMATION
SERVING SIZE: **2 cups of pasta, including 2 chicken sausages**
Calories: 170
Fat: 18 g
Carbohydrates: 19 g
Sodium: 227 mg
Protein: 5 g
Sugar: 2 g

ALSO WORKS WELL WITH
Zucchini

During the week, I'm pretty regular about my breakfast: a green protein smoothie or Greek yogurt with granola and blueberries. But on the weekends it's a totally different ball game. Breakfast becomes brunch, and I can pack in the vegetables and all of my favorite breakfast foods in one shot. This kohlrabi breakfast sauté will change the way you view breakfast. Yes, you can eat noodles for breakfast, and no, I'm not talking about leftover lo mein! Climb out of your own breakfast rut and whip up this dish—your body will be fueled for the day with tons of potassium and dietary fiber. The mild, crunchy kohlrabi perfectly absorbs the flavors of the egg, sausage, and salsa.

For the salsa verde
- 2 medium tomatillos, husks removed, rinsed
- 2 tablespoons fresh lime juice
- Salt
- 2 teaspoons diced jalapeño
- 2 tablespoons chopped white onion
- ¼ cup packed fresh cilantro

To save time, use your favorite canned salsa; just warm it in a small saucepan first.

For the sauté
- Cooking spray
- 2 large eggs, lightly beaten
- 1 tablespoon olive oil
- 4 small apple-flavored chicken breakfast sausages, sliced into ¼-inch-thick rounds
- ⅓ cup diced white onion
- 1 small garlic clove, minced
- 1 large kohlrabi, spiralized with BLADE C
- Salt and pepper
- 2 cups packed chicory (or fresh spinach or arugula)

1 Make the salsa verde. Place the tomatillos in a small saucepan and just cover with water. Bring to a boil over high heat, then reduce to low and simmer for about 10 minutes or until the tomatillos soften and turn light green. Drain in a colander, then place in a food processor along with the lime juice, salt, jalapeño, onion, and cilantro. Blend until the mixture reaches your desired consistency and season to taste.

2 Make the sauté. Place a large nonstick skillet over medium heat and coat with cooking spray. When a bit of water flicked onto the skillet sizzles, add the eggs and scramble until set. Transfer to a bowl.

3 Add the olive oil to the skillet, still over the medium heat. When the oil is shimmering, add the breakfast sausage, onion, and garlic. Cook for 2 to 3 minutes or until the onion is translucent.

4 Add the kohlrabi noodles, season with salt and pepper, and cook for 3 to 5 minutes, tossing frequently, until the noodles soften to al dente. Halfway through the cooking, add the greens and toss to combine.

5 Return the scrambled eggs to the skillet to warm them for about a minute. Divide the mixture evenly between two bowls and drizzle each with the spicy salsa.

SNACKS & SIDES

Spicy Jícama Strings

Cucumber, Avocado, and Strawberry Salsa

Spicy Butternut Squash Nachos

Pears with Farro, Cherries, Walnuts, and Goat Cheese

Lemon Garlic Broccoli with Bacon

Baked Onion Bhaji with Mint-Cucumber Raita

Balsamic Glazed Peaches with Prosciutto and Roquefort

Apple and Kohlrabi Slaw with Lemon-Mint
Chia Seed Dressing

Beet, Goat Cheese, and Pomegranate Endive Cups

Mango-Avocado Cucumber Spring Rolls with
Sriracha-Lime Dipping Sauce

Spicy Jícama Strings

MAKES
5 servings

GF

TIME TO PREPARE
10 minutes

V

TIME TO COOK
25 minutes

P

NUTRITIONAL INFORMATION
SERVING SIZE: ¾ cup
Calories: 108
Fat: 6 g
Carbohydrates: 14 g
Sodium: 16 mg
Protein: 1 g
Sugar: 3 g

ALSO WORKS WELL WITH
Sweet Potatoes ·
Potatoes · Rutabaga ·
Parsnips · Kohlrabi ·
Celeriac

The spiralizer can easily be used to make curly, thick-cut, or shoestring french fries. You can fry them or bake them in the oven to re-create your favorite fast food. But there's nothing special about that, is there? These jícama strings are different, though. I call them "strings" because they're meant to be floppier and not quite as crisp as typical french fries. Most important, they're made with a Mexican root vegetable that's low in sodium and high in fiber—a heavenly combination for those of us looking to eat fries without going up a size. These strings are perfect for topping burgers or salads, or for eating as a side dish!

1 Preheat the oven to 415 degrees. Spread the jícama noodles on two large baking sheets, drizzle with olive oil, and toss to coat well. Season generously with salt, onion powder, cayenne pepper, and chili powder and toss again. Spread in an even layer.

2 Bake for 15 minutes, then flip and bake another 10 to 15 minutes or until the strings reach your preferred crispness.

1 large jícama, peeled, spiralized with BLADE C

2 tablespoons olive oil

Salt

1 tablespoon onion powder

2 teaspoons cayenne pepper

2 teaspoons chili powder

Prior to baking the jícama noodles, be sure to cut them into smaller pieces, no longer than 3 inches. To make these a bit crisper, blanch them for a minute in boiling water, then spread them in an even layer and bake at 450 degrees.

Cucumber, Avocado, and Strawberry Salsa

MAKES
4 to 6 servings

TIME TO PREPARE
15 minutes

NUTRITIONAL INFORMATION
SERVING SIZE: **1 cup**
Calories: 90
Fat: 5 g
Carbohydrates: 14 g
Sodium: 7 mg
Protein: 2 g
Sugar: 7 g

Who says salsa has to have perfectly cubed ingredients? Not those of us who are Inspiralized! It's time to transform your salsas by using cucumber half-moons. Whenever I'm invited to a potluck barbecue or sporting event, where I know healthy foods will be scarce, I bring this filling snack. Not only is it fun to eat, but it's also a conversation starter.

1 Slice the cucumber lengthwise halfway through. Spiralize using blade C. Pat the cucumber noodles dry to absorb moisture.

2 In a large bowl, combine the cucumber noodles, strawberries, avocado, cilantro, jalapeño, and red onion. In a small bowl, whisk together the honey and lime juice and season with salt and pepper. Pour the dressing over the salsa and toss with the cucumber mixture to combine. Serve with chips or vegetable crudités.

1 large seedless cucumber

1½ cups hulled and chopped fresh strawberries

1 very ripe avocado, diced

1 tablespoon chopped fresh cilantro

1 small jalapeño, seeded and finely chopped

⅓ cup finely chopped red onion

1 teaspoon honey

Juice of 1 lime

Salt and pepper

If you're preparing this salsa in advance, add the cucumber noodles at the last minute to avoid a buildup of moisture.

Spicy Butternut Squash Nachos

MAKES
4 to 6 servings

GF

VT

TIME TO PREPARE
25 minutes

TIME TO COOK
35 minutes

NUTRITIONAL INFORMATION
SERVING SIZE: 2 cups
Calories: 246
Fat: 9 g
Carbohydrates: 36 g
Sodium: 204 mg
Protein: 8 g
Sugar: 7 g

ALSO WORKS WELL WITH
Sweet Potatoes ·
Beets

Whenever my parents would visit me in college, my father would insist that we eat at The Village Tavern, a local restaurant. Why? He was crazy for their nachos. Those nachos were beyond fully loaded and worth every bite. By the time we were done with dinner, though, we each were yearning to go lie belly-up on a couch. This slimmed-down version induces that same "Yes, nachos!" feeling without the subsequent bloat. The butternut squash chips replace the corn tortilla chips, and they nourish you while providing that salty crunch. Even my father approves!

For the chips
1 small to medium butternut squash, peeled

Olive oil, for brushing

Salt and pepper

1 teaspoon chili powder

For the topping
1 ear of corn, shucked and silks removed

Olive oil, for brushing

Salt and pepper

½ teaspoon chili powder

For the avocado salsa
1 cup cubed avocado

2 ripe tomatoes, seeded and chopped

1 jalapeño, seeded and finely chopped

1 small white onion, diced

2 tablespoons chopped fresh cilantro

1 tablespoon lime juice

Salt and pepper

For the bean topping
2 teaspoons olive oil

1 small garlic clove, minced

1 cup canned pinto beans, drained and rinsed

½ cup quartered black olives

½ teaspoon ground cumin

¼ teaspoon dried Mexican oregano

¼ cup shredded Monterey Jack cheese

¼ cup shredded sharp Cheddar cheese

Using a small to medium butternut squash will yield the perfect chip size. A larger butternut squash will give you wider, larger slices, which won't work as well in this dish.

1 Make the chips. Preheat the oven to 375 degrees. Line two baking sheets with parchment paper and set aside. Bring a medium pot of salted water to a boil.

2 Cut the squash lengthwise in half and spiralize using blade A. Drop the slices into the boiling water and cook for exactly 2 minutes. Drain and pat dry to remove excess moisture. Arrange the slices in an even layer on one of the baking sheets and brush both sides with olive oil. Season generously with salt, pepper, and chili powder and toss to combine. Bake for 25 to 30 minutes or until crisp, turning halfway through and taking care not to burn the chips.

3 Prepare the corn. Brush the corn with a little olive oil and sprinkle with salt and pepper and the chili powder. Bake the corn for 12 minutes or until it turns deep yellow. Remove the corn from the oven and allow it to cool for a few minutes before slicing the kernels off the cob.

4 Make the salsa. Combine the ingredients in a medium bowl.

5 Prepare the bean topping. Heat the olive oil in a large nonstick skillet over medium heat. When the oil is shimmering, add the garlic and cook for 30 seconds or until fragrant. Add the beans, olives, cumin, and oregano. Cook for 2 to 3 minutes, stirring frequently, or until the beans break down slightly and the vegetables have warmed through. Transfer the bean mixture to a medium bowl and toss in the corn kernels.

6 When the chips are crisp, remove the baking sheet from the oven, but leave the oven on. Place half the chips in the bottom of a large baking dish. Layer over half of the bean topping, then the remaining chips. Finish with the remaining bean topping and sprinkle evenly with the cheeses. Put the baking dish in the oven and bake for 10 to 15 minutes or until the cheese melts. Remove from the oven, top with the avocado salsa, and serve immediately.

Pears with Farro, Cherries, Walnuts, and Goat Cheese

MAKES
3 to 4 servings

VT

TIME TO PREPARE
10 minutes

TIME TO COOK
20 minutes

NUTRITIONAL INFORMATION
SERVING SIZE: **2 cups**
Calories: 348
Fat: 18 g
Carbohydrates: 42 g
Sodium: 136 mg
Protein: 8 g
Sugar: 17 g

Despite the fact that this cookbook is devoted to vegetable substitutes for rice and noodles, that doesn't mean I never eat grains. On the contrary! Farro is one of my favorites, with its pleasant chewiness and lovely nutty flavor. The creaminess of the goat cheese and the sweetness of the cherries and pear noodles complement its al dente texture. I always keep a bag of farro on hand, and I love mixing it into salads and vegetable dishes. My grandfather introduced me to farro, claiming that it fed the Roman Legions. If it's okay for the Romans, it's okay for me!

1 Bring the water to a boil in a large saucepan over high heat. Add the farro and a pinch of salt. Cook for 15 minutes or until the farro is al dente. Drain well.

2 Place the walnuts in a medium nonstick skillet over medium heat and toast for 2 to 3 minutes or until fragrant and lightly browned.

3 Make the dressing. Pulse all the ingredients in a food processor until emulsified and evenly incorporated.

4 Combine the farro, pear noodles, walnuts, and cherries in a large bowl. Pour the dressing on top and toss to combine. Transfer to a serving bowl and top with the goat cheese.

4 cups water
1 cup uncooked farro
   Salt
½ cup chopped walnuts

For the dressing
1 tablespoon honey
1 tablespoon balsamic vinegar
   Salt and pepper
2 tablespoons olive oil
2 tablespoons lemon juice
1 tablespoon whole-grain or country-style Dijon mustard
2 teaspoons minced fresh parsley

2 medium Bosc pears, spiralized with BLADE C
1 cup pitted and halved fresh cherries (Bing or Dark Hudson)
⅓ cup crumbled goat cheese

If you're grain-free, substitute shredded chard or spinach for the farro.

Lemon Garlic Broccoli with Bacon

MAKES
4 servings

GF

TIME TO PREPARE
5 minutes

TIME TO COOK
15 minutes

NUTRITIONAL INFORMATION
SERVING SIZE: **1 heaping cup**
Calories: 305
Fat: 12 g
Carbohydrates: 33 g
Sodium: 332 mg
Protein: 16 g
Sugar: 8 g

ALSO WORKS WELL WITH
Zucchini

My grandfather makes an unbelievably simple dish with garlic, olive oil, and broccoli. Basically, the broccoli floats in a pool of olive oil; when you pierce a floret with your fork, you have to let it drip-dry for a moment before eating it! As much as I love his version, it always leaves me with a slight tummy ache. This recipe brings in extra flavor from the bacon while minimizing the amount of olive oil. Also, it uses the entire broccoli, stem and all! It's a recipe that showcases the extreme versatility of the spiralizer and what it empowers you to make out of everyday vegetables.

1 Fill a large saucepan halfway with salted water and bring to a boil over high heat. Add the broccoli florets and broccoli noodles. Cook for 2 to 3 minutes or until easily pierced with a fork. Drain and pat dry.

2 Place a large skillet over medium heat and coat with cooking spray. When water flicked onto the skillet sizzles, add the bacon slices in an even layer, working in batches if needed, and cook for 3 minutes per side or until browned and crisp to your liking. Set aside on a paper towel–lined plate to drain.

3 Wipe out the skillet, return it to medium heat, and add the olive oil. When the oil is shimmering, add the broccoli florets, broccoli noodles, and red pepper flakes; season with salt and pepper. Cover and cook for 2 minutes, uncovering occasionally to toss. Add the garlic, lemon juice, and zest; cover and cook for another 5 minutes or until the broccoli is lightly browned.

4 Remove the pan from the heat and stir in the cheese. Toss to combine and serve warm.

3 large broccoli heads with stems (see Tip)

Cooking spray

6 bacon slices

2 tablespoons olive oil

¼ teaspoon red pepper flakes
Salt and pepper

5 medium garlic cloves, thinly sliced
Juice of 1 lemon and zest of half a lemon

3 tablespoons grated Parmesan cheese

Slice off the broccoli florets, leaving as little stem as possible, and set aside. Then spiralize the stems using blade C.

Baked Onion Bhaji with Mint-Cucumber Raita

MAKES
4 to 6 bhajis

GF

VT

TIME TO PREPARE
15 minutes

TIME TO COOK
45 minutes

NUTRITIONAL INFORMATION
**SERVING SIZE: 1 bhaji and
2 tablespoons of raita**
Calories: 91
Fat: 3 g
Carbohydrates: 9 g
Sodium: 30 mg
Protein: 5 g
Sugar: 4 g

ALSO WORKS WELL WITH
Potatoes

One of the easiest ways to revamp your beloved fried foods is to bake them. The onion bhaji, also sometimes called a pakora, depending on the region, is India's version of a British or American fritter. Typically crispy and sinfully delicious, this Inspiralized version is whipped up quickly using spiralized onions, and because it is baked, it has much less saturated fat. Instead of eliminating unwholesome foods from your diet, you can always find a way to make a cleaner version!

For the bhajis

Cooking spray

1 medium onion, peeled, spiralized with BLADE A

¼ teaspoon chili powder

½ teaspoon ground turmeric

¼ teaspoon ground cumin

¼ teaspoon ground ginger

2 teaspoons minced fresh cilantro

½ cup chickpea flour or coconut flour

1 large egg, lightly beaten

½ tablespoon olive oil

Salt and pepper

2–3 lemons, quartered for use as garnish

For the raita

¼ medium cucumber, chopped

½ cup plain nonfat Greek yogurt

1 teaspoon chopped fresh mint leaves

Salt and pepper

1 teaspoon fresh lemon juice

1 Make the bhaji. Preheat the oven to 400 degrees. Line a baking sheet with parchment paper and coat with cooking spray.

2 Heat a large nonstick skillet over medium heat. When a little water flicked onto the skillet sizzles, add the onion and cook for 3 to 4 minutes or until beginning to turn translucent. Transfer to a bowl to cool for 2 to 3 minutes.

3 In a medium bowl, combine the chili powder, turmeric, cumin, ginger, cilantro, and flour. Add the egg and the onion and mix well. If the mixture appears too dry, gradually add warm water, 1 tablespoon at a time.

4 Working with ¼ cup mixture at a time, transfer the mixture to the parchment paper, using the back of a spatula to flatten into disks. Brush the tops of the bhajis with olive oil and season with salt and pepper. Bake for 40 minutes or until golden brown, flipping halfway through.

5 Prepare your raita. Press out the extra moisture in the cucumber with a paper towel and mince. Add the cucumber to a medium bowl along with the rest of the ingredients and mix well. Season to taste.

6 To serve, squeeze a lemon quarter over each and serve with raita alongside.

For an extra crispy outside on your bhajis, use a cast-iron skillet coated with a tablespoon of olive oil instead of a baking sheet. The olive oil will bubble up and "fry" them in the oven.

Balsamic Glazed Peaches with Prosciutto and Roquefort

MAKES
16 hors d'oeuvres

TIME TO PREPARE
20 minutes

TIME TO COOK
15 minutes

NUTRITIONAL INFORMATION
SERVING SIZE: **1 peach with a drizzle of balsamic glaze and a crumbling of Roquefort**
Calories: 86
Fat: 4 g
Carbohydrates: 6 g
Sodium: 113 mg
Protein: 5 g
Sugar: 6 g

My mother taught me to never arrive at someone's home empty-handed. The polite thing is to bring a bottle of wine or some flowers. But, why not *really* make an impression by walking through the door with these hors d'oeuvres? The prosciutto-wrapped seared peaches are sophisticated, but best for summertime. The zucchini ribbons are purely decorative, but they add color and some fun. Whether you're serving these at your own soiree or bringing them to a friend, they'll be the talk of the evening!

1 Make the glaze. In a small bowl, whisk together the ingredients and pour into a small saucepan. Bring to a boil over high heat, then reduce to low and simmer for 10 to 15 minutes or until thickened and syrupy. Stir occasionally to prevent the glaze from hardening while it cooks.

2 Prepare the peaches. Cut each peach into 8 slices, discarding the pit. Set aside. Snip the zucchini noodles into 16 pieces each 6 inches long. Try to use as much of the zucchini that still has its green skin, and reserve the remainder in an airtight container for later use.

3 Toss the zucchini noodles in a nonstick skillet over medium heat to soften slightly, about 2 minutes. Remove the pan from the heat and set aside.

For the glaze
¾ cup balsamic vinegar
2 tablespoons honey
Salt

For the peaches
2 ripe peaches
2 large zucchini, spiralized with BLADE D
Cooking spray
16 thin slices of prosciutto
½ cup crumbled Roquefort cheese

(recipe continues)

4 Place a grill pan over medium-high heat and spray with cooking spray. When water flicked onto the pan sizzles, add the peaches and sear for 1 minute on each side, until char marks appear.

5 Lay a piece of prosciutto on a clean, flat surface and fold lengthwise to create one long strip. Place one peach slice on the left side of the prosciutto. Crumble about 1 teaspoon of Roquefort over the peach and roll the prosciutto from left to right, until it is completely wrapped around the peach slice. Secure with a toothpick. Repeat with remaining peach slices.

6 Lay a zucchini noodle on a clean, flat surface. Take one wrapped peach and center it on the zucchini. Carefully tie a knot in the zucchini around the peach. Place the knotted peaches on a serving platter and lightly crumble over remaining Roquefort. Drizzle over the balsamic glaze and serve.

Take care not to pull too tightly on the zucchini as you tie it around the peaches—the ribbons snap easily. Instead, pull gently and immediately secure with a toothpick.

Apple and Kohlrabi Slaw with Lemon-Mint Chia Seed Dressing

GF
VT

MAKES
2 servings

TIME TO PREPARE
30 minutes

NUTRITIONAL INFORMATION
SERVING SIZE: **1½–2 cups**
Calories: 323
Fat: 15 g
Carbohydrates: 47 g
Sodium: 52 mg
Protein: 6 g
Sugar: 30 g

ALSO WORKS WELL WITH
Jícama

Chia seeds are from a plant that grows mainly in South America; *chia* is the Mayan word for "strength." Don't be fooled—they're tiny, but they pack a heavy nutritional punch! They're loaded with fiber, antioxidants, and protein, making them ideal for weight loss and for building a strong immune system. Thanks to their high fiber content, they absorb over ten times their weight in water, becoming gel-like and expanding in your stomach, thus helping you feel fuller. With this dressing drizzled over this dazzling slaw, you'll have a tasty way to reap all the benefits of chia.

1 Make the dressing. Soak the chia seeds in the water for at least 30 minutes or overnight.

2 Whisk the rest of the dressing ingredients in a small bowl. Whisk in the soaked chia seeds.

3 Make the slaw. Combine all the ingredients in a medium serving bowl and toss to mix well. Drizzle the slaw with the dressing and serve immediately.

For a different texture, cut the kohlrabi and apple halfway through and use blade B to spiralize it. You'll have half-moon slices that will be heartier and easier to serve.

For the dressing
1 tablespoon chia seeds
½ cup water
½ tablespoon chopped fresh mint
1 tablespoon honey
¼ cup lemon juice
1½ tablespoons olive oil

For the slaw
1 apple, spiralized with BLADE C
1 kohlrabi, peeled, spiralized with BLADE C
¼ cup dried cranberries
¼ cup lightly crushed cashews
1 small carrot, peeled and shaved into strips with a vegetable peeler

Beet, Goat Cheese, and Pomegranate Endive Cups

GF

MAKES
12 hors d'oeuvres

TIME TO PREPARE
20 minutes

TIME TO COOK
5 minutes

NUTRITIONAL INFORMATION
SERVING SIZE: **1 endive cup with ¼ cup of filling**
Calories: 69
Fat: 4 g
Carbohydrates: 4 g
Sodium: 74 mg
Protein: 3 g
Sugar: 3 g

These endive "cups" take very little time to make, but they look elegant and festive. Plus, they're packed with superfoods, and the goat cheese has a creamy sweetness that takes the bite out of the otherwise bitter endive. Just be prepared to share the recipe—these are a crowd-pleaser!

Try to find the biggest Belgian endive as possible so that you'll have large leaves to pack in the filling.

1 In a small bowl, whisk together the vinegar, olive oil, honey, and salt and pepper.

2 Place the beet rice in a medium bowl and toss with the goat cheese, pomegranate seeds, and dressing.

3 Separate the endive and select 12 large leaves to serve as cups. Fill each leaf with the beet mixture, then transfer to a large plate or platter and serve.

2 teaspoons white balsamic vinegar

2 teaspoons olive oil

2 teaspoons honey
  Salt and pepper

2 large golden beets, peeled, spiralized with BLADE C, then riced (see page 25)

1 cup crumbled goat cheese

½ cup pomegranate seeds

4 large Belgian endive

Mango-Avocado Cucumber Spring Rolls with Sriracha-Lime Dipping Sauce

My first job out of college was in event and hotel management at a golf club that was a 45-minute drive from where I lived at the time. When I worked on weekends, I'd stop on my way out there at my favorite grocery store and pick up some spring rolls just like these. I'd stuff them into the fridge when I got there, work a full day, and then eat them on my ride home—a fresh, crunchy treat. The combination of sweet mango and mashed avocado is heavenly, especially with the spicy lime dipping sauce. The cucumber noodles add unexpected crunch, too. Here's my at-home version of those spring rolls.

1 In a medium bowl, combine the avocado with the salt, pepper, lime juice, cilantro, and mango.

2 Make the dipping sauce. Whisk the ingredients in a medium bowl. Transfer to a serving bowl and place in the refrigerator to chill until ready to serve.

3 Fill a large bowl with warm water. Working with one piece at a time, submerge a rice paper wrapper in the water for a few seconds just until softened, then lay on a clean, flat surface. Across the center, leaving about 2 inches of space on each side, place a layer of the chard, then top with about ⅓ cup of the avocado mixture, and finish with a handful of cucumber noodles. Fold the uncovered sides inward and then tightly roll up the wrapper lengthwise. Repeat with the remaining ingredients and remaining wrappers.

4 Slice each roll in half and pierce each half with a toothpick. Serve with the dipping sauce alongside.

1 avocado, mashed
  Salt and pepper
1 tablespoon lime juice
1 tablespoon finely chopped fresh cilantro
1 small mango, cubed

For the dipping sauce
¼ cup soy sauce
2 tablespoons lime juice
2 tablespoons honey
2 tablespoons Sriracha or other hot sauce
  Salt and pepper

6 rice papers for spring rolls
1 cup chopped rainbow chard or other green
1 medium cucumber, spiralized with BLADE C

SOUPS, STEWS & SALADS

Chicken Carrot Noodle Soup

Ginger Scallion Egg Drop Bowl

Cajun Beef and Celeriac Chili

Daikon Ramen with Skirt Steak

Shrimp Daikon Pho

Steak and Pear Kale Salad

Caprese Zucchini Salad

Avocado-Lime Mason Jar Salad

Jícama, Kiwi, and Corn Salad with Honey-Mint Dressing

Pear, Fontina, and Fig Salad with Honey-Pistachio Dressing

Pickled Onion and Watermelon Salad with Ricotta Salata

Apples with Shaved Asparagus, Gorgonzola, and Pecans

Tomatokeftedes and Cauliflower Tabouleh Salad

Cucumber Noodle Salad with Feta, Arugula, and
Red Wine Vinaigrette

Italian Zucchini Pasta Salad

Chicken Carrot Noodle Soup

MAKES
2 to 3 servings

GF

TIME TO PREPARE
25 minutes

P

TIME TO COOK
15 minutes

NUTRITIONAL INFORMATION
SERVING SIZE: 2.5 cups
Calories: 212
Fat: 11 g
Carbohydrates: 6 g
Sodium: 1056 mg
Protein: 23 g
Sugar: 2 g

ALSO WORKS WELL WITH
Daikon Radish ·
Kohlrabi · Broccoli
Stems · Celeriac ·
Sweet Potatoes ·
Butternut Squash

Instead of adding chopped carrots to this classic, why not use the carrots as a substitute for egg noodles? They offer a subtle crunch, which complements the simplicity of the preparation. Everyone needs a little comfort every once in a while, and this soup provides exactly that, without the starch or accompanying bloat. Small changes like this yield big results.

1 Heat the olive oil in a large saucepan over medium heat. When the oil is shimmering, add the garlic, celery, and onion. Season with salt and pepper and cook, stirring, for 3 to 5 minutes, or until the onion is translucent and the vegetables begin to soften.

2 Add the broth, thyme, oregano, and parsley. Increase the heat to high and bring to a boil, then reduce to low and simmer for 5 minutes. Add the chicken and carrot noodles. Cook for about 5 minutes, or until the noodles soften, and serve.

2 tablespoons olive oil

1½ large garlic cloves, minced

2 celery stalks, halved lengthwise and chopped

½ medium white onion, chopped

Salt and pepper

4 cups low-sodium chicken broth

4 thyme sprigs

½ teaspoon dried oregano

1 teaspoon chopped fresh parsley

1½ to 2 cups shredded rotisserie chicken

1 large carrot, peeled, spiralized with BLADE A

If you want to mimic the traditional wide egg noodles, substitute zucchini noodles using blade A. Add them at the very end, cooking for just 2 to 3 minutes or until al dente.

Ginger Scallion Egg Drop Soup

MAKES
1 serving

TIME TO PREPARE
10 minutes

TIME TO COOK
15 minutes

NUTRITIONAL INFORMATION
SERVING SIZE: to come
Calories: 243
Fat: 15 g
Carbohydrates: 15 g
Sodium: 2577
Protein: 10 g
Sugar: 9 g

ALSO WORKS WELL WITH
Daikon Radish ·
Kohlrabi

On one of our first dates, Lu brought me to the Momofuku noodle bar, in New York City's East Village. At the time I wasn't eating meat, and everything on the menu seemed to contain crispy pork belly or sausage. Then, my eyes landed on the ginger scallion noodles. It could've been the giddiness of being with Lu, but I was blown away by how flavorful this simple dish was. Later, I wanted to add some protein to my version, so I turned it into a half egg drop soup, half ginger scallion noodles. As this recipe shows, every moment is an opportunity to Inspiralize something great.

1 Heat the oil in a large saucepan over medium heat. When the oil is shimmering, add the ginger and cook for 1 minute, stirring frequently. Increase the heat to high and add the red pepper flakes, sherry vinegar, soy sauce, broth, and water.

2 Bring the broth to a boil, then add the seaweed. Slowly pour in the egg while rapidly stirring. Add the zucchini noodles, scallions, and pepper, and cook for about 2 minutes or until the noodles are cooked through but still crisp. Transfer to a bowl and serve.

¾ tablespoon canola oil

1 tablespoon minced fresh ginger

¼ teaspoon red pepper flakes

2 teaspoons sherry vinegar

1 tablespoon low-sodium soy sauce

2 cups vegetable broth

½ cup water

3 tablespoons dried seaweed ribbons

1 large egg, lightly beaten

½ large zucchini, spiralized with BLADE C

½ cup chopped scallion, green and white parts

Freshly ground pepper

The faster you whisk the egg into the broth, the wispier it will get. If you want larger egg wisps, whisk slowly.

Cajun Beef Celeriac Chili

MAKES
4 servings

GF

P

TIME TO PREPARE
15 minutes

TIME TO COOK
25 minutes

NUTRITIONAL INFORMATION
SERVING SIZE: **1½–2 cups**
Calories: 253
Fat: 10 g
Carbohydrates: 15 g
Sodium: 228 mg
Protein: 27 g
Sugar: 7 g

ALSO WORKS WELL WITH
Sweet Potatoes ·
Butternut Squash ·
Rutabaga

I could eat turkey chili with brown rice on every rainy, cold day in the fall. This recipe takes it up a notch, with celeriac rice instead. It offers familiar texture, but also a fresh, earthy taste that helps combat the heaviness of the beef—plus it squeezes extra nutrients into your meal. Save this one for those chilly days when you're craving something filling and warm.

1 Heat the olive oil in large saucepan over medium heat. When the oil is shimmering, add the onion, garlic, and red pepper flakes and cook for 30 seconds or until fragrant. Add the beef, breaking it up with a wooden spoon, and cook for 3 to 5 minutes more, or until browned.

2 Add the celeriac rice, tomatoes, broth, cumin, cayenne, chili powder, onion powder, oregano, paprika, bay leaf, salt, and pepper, and stir to combine. Cover and cook for 10 minutes, then uncover and continue cooking for an additional 5 to 10 minutes or until the chili is thick and the celeriac has softened.

3 Remove the pan from the heat, discard the bay leaf, then sprinkle with parsley and serve hot.

1 tablespoon olive oil

½ cup diced white onion

1 tablespoon minced garlic

¼ teaspoon red pepper flakes

1 pound lean ground beef

1 large celeriac, peeled, spiralized with BLADE C, then riced (see page 25)

2 (14-ounce) cans diced tomatoes, no salt added

½ cup low-sodium beef broth

2 teaspoons ground cumin

½ teaspoon cayenne pepper

½ teaspoon chili powder

½ teaspoon onion powder

1 teaspoon dried oregano

¼ teaspoon smoked paprika

1 bay leaf

Salt and pepper

1 tablespoon minced fresh parsley

Daikon Ramen with Skirt Steak

MAKES
2 servings

TIME TO PREPARE
10 minutes

TIME TO COOK
20 minutes

NUTRITIONAL INFORMATION
**SERVING SIZE: 3 cups with
2 ounces of skirt steak**
Calories: 391
Fat: 26 g
Carbohydrates: 11 g
Sodium: 1265 mg
Protein: 28 g
Sugar: 6 g

ALSO WORKS WELL WITH
Zucchini · Turnips ·
Kohlrabi · Chayote ·
Carrots

This noodle dish has the consistency and flavor profile of ramen noodles without the, well, ramen. Don't get me wrong, I used to eat the instant stuff in college; it's salty and addictively tasty, but has the nutritional value of cardboard. Whenever you eat, it's important to ask yourself, "Is this food going to make me feel good? Is it what my body needs to get me through the day?" If the answer is no, ditch it. By swapping in the daikon here, you're replacing the empty noodles with a root vegetable that's rich in vitamin C and low in calories and carbohydrates. If I had only known in college!

1 Slice the thick white stems off the bok choy and then chop the green leaves in half.

2 Coat the steak with hoisin sauce and generously season with salt and pepper. Heat a large skillet over medium heat and add the olive oil. When the oil is shimmering, add the steak and cook for 2 to 3 minutes on each side, or until it reaches your desired doneness; keep in mind that the steak will cook slightly more once it is removed from the heat. Set the steak on a cutting board.

3 Place a large pot over medium heat and add the vegetable oil. When the oil is shimmering, add the garlic, ginger, and scallions. Cook for 30 seconds, until fragrant, then add the mushrooms and the bok choy. Cook for 3 to 4 minutes, or until the mushrooms are softened.

1 bunch bok choy

4 ounces boneless skirt steak

1 tablespoon hoisin sauce
   Salt and pepper

1 tablespoon olive oil

1 tablespoon vegetable oil

1 teaspoon minced garlic

½ teaspoon minced fresh ginger

⅓ cup sliced scallions, green and white parts

1 cup shiitake mushrooms

2 cups vegetable broth

1 cup water

2 teaspoons low-sodium soy sauce

1 medium daikon radish, peeled, spiralized with BLADE C

2 hard-boiled eggs, halved

4 Add the broth, water, and soy sauce. Increase the heat to high and bring to a boil. Reduce the heat to low, and add the daikon noodles. Cook for 2 minutes, or until the noodles are al dente.

5 Thinly slice the steak against the grain. Serve the ramen in portions topped with steak slices and the egg halves.

Shrimp Daikon Pho

MAKES
2 servings

GF

TIME TO PREPARE
20 minutes

TIME TO COOK
15 minutes

NUTRITIONAL INFORMATION
SERVING SIZE: **2 cups of soup with 6 shrimp**
Calories: 87
Fat: 1 g
Carbohydrates: 11 g
Sodium: 2165 mg
Protein: 9 g
Sugar: 4 g

ALSO WORKS WELL WITH
Zucchini · Kohlrabi ·
Jícama · Chayote

One weekend I was walking through Hoboken, and I saw a new restaurant called Pho-nomenal. (Let's just say that when you start with the "pho" jokes, you can't stop. Pho-gettabout it. Pho-shizzle. Pho real.) Pho—pronounced "fuh"—is a flavorful Vietnamese street food that varies in sweetness and noodle type. I've adapted and simplified the traditional dish by replacing the rice noodles with daikon noodles for a lighter, spicier version.

1 Place a large soup pot over medium heat and add the broth, water, fish sauce, lime juice, coriander, and ginger. Season with salt and pepper, increase the heat to high, bring to a boil, and add the shrimp. Reduce the heat to medium-low and cook at a strong simmer for about 5 minutes, or until shrimp are cooked through and opaque.

2 Add the daikon noodles and cilantro, stir to combine, and cook for about 2 minutes more, until the daikon noodles are softened.

3 Serve the pho hot, garnished with the scallions, jalapeños, onion slices, and hot sauce, if desired.

This pho base can be customized to your preference by using beef, chicken, or tofu—all common pho proteins.

3 cups vegetable broth

2 cups water

2 teaspoons Vietnamese or Thai fish sauce

3 tablespoons fresh lime juice

1 teaspoon ground coriander

1 teaspoon minced fresh ginger

Salt and pepper

12 small shrimp, peeled and deveined, defrosted if frozen

1 large daikon radish, peeled, spiralized with BLADE C

¼ cup packed whole cilantro leaves

2 to 3 scallions, green and white parts diced

2 small jalapeños (or 1 large), seeded and thinly sliced crosswise

2 thin slices white onion

Sriracha or other hot sauce (optional)

Steak and Pear Kale Salad

MAKES
2 servings

GF

TIME TO PREPARE
20 minutes

TIME TO COOK
10 minutes

NUTRITIONAL INFORMATION
SERVING SIZE: **3 cups of salad with 2 ounces of steak**
Calories: 525
Fat: 39 g
Carbohydrates: 28 g
Sodium: 495 mg
Protein: 20 g
Sugar: 6 g

ALSO WORKS WELL WITH
Apples

When I first started putting meat back into my diet after my vegan years, the only way I could stomach red meat was in a salad. New to cooking meat, I spent countless nights in my kitchen, searing steak until it was cooked to my preference: well done with the slightest hint of pink. I would flip the steaks, slice them open, and find that they were either underdone or as firm as hockey pucks. Luckily, even if the steak didn't turn out well, the salad beneath it was prepared to perfection. But finally I mastered the art. This kale salad enhances the flavor of the steak atop it, and will tantalize your taste buds with every crunchy forkful.

1 Prepare the salad. Whisk the honey, oil, vinegar, salt and pepper, mustard, shallot, and water in a large bowl. Add the kale, toss to combine, and set in the refrigerator to soften.

2 Make the steak. Pat the steak dry and season generously with salt and pepper on both sides. Heat a cast-iron skillet over medium-high heat and add the olive oil. When the oil is shimmering, add the steak and cook 3 to 4 minutes per side. Remove the steak from the heat and allow it to rest for 5 minutes. Cut the meat against the grain into thin slices.

3 Add the pear noodles to the dressed kale and mix well. Place the salad on plates and top with steak slices, then crumble on the blue cheese.

If you don't like blue cheese, substitute flakes or shavings of Parmigiano-Reggiano, or just omit it altogether.

For the salad
2 teaspoons honey
3 tablespoons olive oil
2 tablespoons red wine vinegar
Salt and pepper
2 teaspoons Dijon mustard
1 shallot, minced
1 tablespoon water
2 packed cups chopped curly kale

For the steak
4 ounces boneless beef steak (sirloin or strip)
Salt and pepper
1 tablespoon olive oil
1 large Bosc pear, spiralized with BLADE C
⅓ cup crumbled blue cheese

Caprese Zucchini Salad

MAKES
2 to 3 servings

TIME TO PREPARE
20 minutes

NUTRITIONAL INFORMATION
SERVING SIZE: 2 cups
Calories: 216
Fat: 17 g
Carbohydrates: 7 g
Sodium: 40 mg
Protein: 9 g
Sugar: 5 g

Thinking back to those late-afternoon dinners at my grandparents' house in the summer, I can't recall a single time when my grandfather didn't make a caprese salad. This traditional Italian dish is defined by the freshness of the tomatoes and basil and the quality of the olive oil and mozzarella. When you hit all of those points, the salad can't be anything but extraordinary. Balsamic vinegar and lemon juice transform the basics into a perfect salad for a summer evening.

1 Place the zucchini and tomatoes in a large bowl.

2 Make the marinade. Pulse the ingredients in a food processor until the garlic is smooth.

3 Pour the marinade over the zucchini noodles and tomatoes, and toss to combine. Place in the refrigerator to marinate for at least 10 minutes.

4 Add the mozzarella and basil to the zucchini noodles, toss to combine, and serve.

2 medium zucchini, spiralized with **BLADE A**, then noodles trimmed to **5 inches or less**

¾ cup cherry tomatoes, halved

For the marinade
1 tablespoon lemon juice
3 tablespoons balsamic vinegar
2 tablespoons olive oil
1 medium garlic clove, minced
Salt and pepper

12 small mozzarella balls, halved
½ cup thinly sliced basil leaves

The longer the zucchini marinates, the more intense the flavors will be, so don't be afraid to prepare this salad in advance.

Avocado-Lime Mason Jar Salad

MAKES
4 servings

GF

TIME TO PREPARE
15 minutes

TIME TO COOK
15 minutes

NUTRITIONAL INFORMATION
SERVING SIZE: **1 pint salad**
Calories: 331
Fat: 24 g
Carbohydrates: 18 g
Sodium: 90 mg
Protein: 16 g
Sugar: 6 g

ALSO WORKS WELL WITH
Jícama · Chayote ·
Kohlrabi · Carrots ·
Beets

If you're not eating dairy, using avocado to thicken your dressings for pasta salads is a handy trick. Avocados are not only tasty but also a powerful source of healthy monosaturated fat, which is especially important in a low-carb diet. This salad is full of protein and Mexican-inspired flavor. The olives, cilantro, and lime juice add tanginess and freshness to the zucchini noodles. It's appropriate for a summertime barbecue or a lean weeknight meal. You'll need four pint-size Mason jars. Just pour the jars into bowls when you're ready to eat!

1 Heat the olive oil in a large nonstick skillet over medium heat. When the oil is shimmering, add the chicken and season with salt and pepper. Cook for 6 to 8 minutes, until lightly browned on the outside and no longer pink on the inside.

2 Place the corn in a medium saucepan over high heat, cover with water, and add a pinch of salt. Bring to a boil and cook for 2 to 3 minutes, or until the corn is easily pierced with a fork. Drain and, when cooled to the touch, slice the kernels off the cobs.

3 Make the dressing. Combine the cilantro, garlic, salt and pepper, olive oil, lime juice, and avocado in a food processor and pulse until creamy. One tablespoon at a time, add some room-temperature water until the dressing reaches the desired consistency, pulsing after every addition.

1 tablespoon olive oil

8 ounces boneless chicken, cut into ½-inch dice

Salt and pepper

2 ears of corn, husked and silks removed

For the dressing

2 to 3 tablespoons chopped fresh cilantro

1 medium garlic clove, minced

Salt and pepper

3 tablespoons olive oil

2 tablespoons lime juice

1 avocado, cubed

½ large red bell pepper, diced

¾ cup halved black olives

3 medium zucchini, spiralized with BLADE C

4 Place a quarter of the dressing at the bottom of four 1-pint Mason jars and add a serving of chicken. Then layer in the bell pepper, olives, and the corn kernels. Finally, top each jar with some of the zucchini noodles. Place tops on the jars and refrigerate for up to 1 day or serve at room temperature within 3 hours.

Avocado browns quickly, so if you're making this dish in advance, prepare everything except the dressing. Assemble the dressing right before serving.

Jícama, Kiwi, and Corn Salad with Honey-Mint Dressing

MAKES
3 servings

TIME TO PREPARE
15 minutes

TIME TO COOK
10 minutes

NUTRITIONAL INFORMATION
SERVING SIZE: 2.5 cups
Calories: 246
Fat: 5 g
Carbohydrates: 49 g
Sodium: 17 mg
Protein: 3 g
Sugar: 25 g

What makes this particular jícama salad special is the honey-mint dressing—you'll be licking the bowl clean afterward. The combination of kiwi and corn offers a crunchy sweetness that's amplified by the mint dressing. This salad pairs especially well with freshly grilled fish.

1 Place the corn in a medium saucepan over high heat, cover with water, and add a pinch of salt. Bring to a boil and cook for 2 minutes, or until the corn is easily pierced with a fork. Drain and let cool, then slice the kernels off the cob.

2 Make the dressing. Whisk together the mint, olive oil, water, honey, vinegar, lime juice, and salt and pepper in a large bowl.

3 Add the corn kernels, the jícama, kiwis, and lettuce to the bowl with the dressing. Toss to combine thoroughly, then transfer to a serving bowl.

1 large ear corn, husked and silks removed

For the dressing
1 tablespoon chopped fresh mint
1 tablespoon olive oil
1 tablespoon water
2 tablespoons honey
2 tablespoons white balsamic vinegar
2 teaspoons lime juice
Salt and pepper

1 medium jícama, peeled, spiralized with BLADE C
3 kiwifruits, peeled and cubed
1 head Bibb lettuce, roughly chopped

If you make this salad in advance, combine all the ingredients except the lettuce. Allow the salad to sit for a few hours so the jícama softens as it absorbs the dressing.

Pear, Fontina, and Fig Salad with Honey-Pistachio Balsamic

GF

VT

MAKES
3 to 4 servings

TIME TO PREPARE
20 minutes

NUTRITIONAL INFORMATION
SERVING SIZE: 3 cups
Calories: 273
Fat: 16 g
Carbohydrates: 29 g
Sodium: 235 mg
Protein: 7 g
Sugar: 21 g

ALSO WORKS WELL WITH
Apples

Lu and I have an ongoing debate about which of our favorite neighborhood restaurants has the best cheese plate. We both love having a good charcuterie and cheese board on Friday night, after a long week. I wanted to re-create those flavors in a recipe. With its boldness, this salad can be a stand-alone meal or it can be served alongside a juicy steak or grilled chicken breast.

1 Make the dressing. Pulse the ingredients in a food processor until fully combined.

2 Prepare the salad. Combine the pear noodles, chard, and figs in a large bowl.

3 Toss the noodles with the dressing and serve, topped with fontina strips and pistachios.

To shred the chard, cut away the tough white stems. Roll up the leafy parts like a cigar and cut into ⅛-inch slices. When you're finished, the chard will be shredded. This trick works for basil, too!

For the dressing
⅓ cup balsamic vinegar
2 tablespoons olive oil
2 tablespoons honey
Black pepper

For the salad
2 Bosc or Anjou pears, spiralized with BLADE C
3 cups shredded chard (see Tip)
½ cup quartered fresh figs
About 20 pieces fontina cheese, in ¼-inch-thick matchsticks
¼ cup roasted and salted pistachios

Pickled Onion and Watermelon Salad with Ricotta Salata

MAKES
3 servings

TIME TO PREPARE
25 minutes

TIME TO COOK
10 minutes

NUTRITIONAL INFORMATION
SERVING SIZE: **1 heaping cup with a few shavings of ricotta salata**
Calories: 119
Fat: 3 g
Carbohydrates: 21 g
Sodium: 17 mg
Protein: 3 g
Sugar: 17 g

There's nothing like sitting outside, watching the summer sun go down, and sipping a glass of wine or iced tea. What could possibly make the scene better? A tasty snack! This refreshing salad is sure to hit the spot. The ricotta salata adds hard texture and provides a kick of flavor. Most important, the pickled onions are long and twirly—fun to eat and an impressive presentation!

1 In a medium bowl, combine the vinegar, onion noodles, honey, and salt. Let marinate in the refrigerator for 15 to 20 minutes.

2 Combine the watermelon and mint in a large bowl. Add the pickled onion noodles and toss. Transfer to a serving bowl and top with the ricotta salata.

¼ **cup red wine vinegar**

1 small red onion, peeled, spiralized with BLADE A

1 tablespoon honey

Pinch of salt

3 cups cubed watermelon

1 tablespoon fresh mint leaves

Shavings of ricotta salata

Apples with Shaved Asparagus, Gorgonzola, and Pecans

GF

VT

MAKES
2 servings

TIME TO PREPARE
15 minutes

NUTRITIONAL INFORMATION
SERVING SIZE: **2.5 heaping cups**
Calories: 316
Fat: 24 g
Carbohydrates: 21 g
Sodium: 265 mg
Protein: 7 g
Sugar: 16 g

Sometimes you just need a salad. Before I left corporate America, I'd buy one every day for lunch. But the ingredients were so predictable—raw or steamed veggies, sliced fruits, diced proteins. Now you can keep your salads interesting by adding fruit noodles! This salad tastes gourmet and looks fancy, too, with its rich cheese, crunchy pecans, and dainty shaved asparagus. Every bite is exciting!

1 Make the dressing. Whisk the ingredients in a medium bowl. Taste and adjust the seasoning.

2 Prepare the salad. Using a vegetable peeler, thinly shave each asparagus spear. In a large bowl, combine the shaved asparagus, the watercress, pecans, and apple noodles.

3 Drizzle with the vinaigrette, toss to combine, and serve topped with the Gorgonzola.

For the dressing
- 1 tablespoon honey
- 1 tablespoon olive oil
- 1 tablespoon red wine vinegar
- 2 teaspoons Dijon mustard
- 1 tablespoon water
- 3 teaspoons minced shallot
- Salt and pepper

For the salad
- 10 large asparagus spears, tough ends snapped off
- 1 cup packed watercress
- ⅓ cup roughly chopped pecans
- 1 apple, spiralized with BLADE C
- ¼ cup crumbled Gorgonzola cheese

For a protein boost, add thinly sliced steak, grilled chicken, or quinoa.

Tomatokeftedes and Cauliflower Tabouleh Salad

MAKES
2 to 3 servings

GF

VT

TIME TO PREPARE
35 minutes

TIME TO COOK
20 minutes

NUTRITIONAL INFORMATION
SERVING SIZE: **2 cups**
Calories: 170
Fat: 6 g
Carbohydrates: 24 g
Sodium: 313 mg
Protein: 9 g
Sugar: 7 g

ALSO WORKS WELL WITH
Zucchini · Kohlrabi ·
Chayote · Jícama

The first getaway trip Lu and I took together as a couple was to Santorini and Mykonos, in Greece. When we arrived at our hotel on Santorini, it was late at night, but we were ravenous from almost 20 hours of traveling. We dropped our bags and walked a few minutes to a small nearby spot and asked for "anything Santorinian." The waitress brought us tomatokeftedes—fried tomato balls. I don't know if it was the exhaustion or the excitement, but I will never forget that first bite. Of course, we devoured them and ordered more. For the rest of our stay on Santorini we never ate at a restaurant without ordering their tomatokeftedes. These healthy tomato balls are my way of bringing a bit of Santorini to you.

For the tomatokeftedes
- Cooking spray
- 1 cup chopped small cherry tomatoes
- ½ cup chopped scallion, green and white parts
- 1 tablespoon warm water
- 1 tablespoon chopped fresh mint
- ¼ teaspoon dried oregano
- ¼ cup whole wheat or chickpea flour
- ¼ cup grated pecorino romano cheese
- Salt and pepper

For the tabouleh
- 1 large seedless cucumber, spiralized with BLADE C
- 1 cup cauliflower florets
- ½ cup finely diced red onion
- 3 tablespoons chopped fresh flat-leaf parsley
- 1 tablespoon chopped fresh mint
- Salt and pepper
- 3 tablespoons lemon juice
- Zest of half a lemon

For the tzatziki
- ¼ cup plain nonfat Greek yogurt
- 1 medium garlic clove, finely minced
- ¼ tablespoon olive oil
- ¼ tablespoon red wine vinegar
- ½ tablespoon chopped fresh dill
- ¾ tablespoon lemon juice
- Salt and pepper

(recipe continues)

1 Preheat the oven to 400 degrees. Line a baking sheet with parchment paper and coat the paper with cooking spray.

2 Make the tomatokeftedes. In a large bowl, add all the ingredients. Using your hands to partially crush the tomatoes, combine the ingredients until the mixture is thick and sticky. (If needed, add more flour and/or water.) Form tomatokeftedes about the size of a golf ball; you should have about 6. Place them on the baking sheet and press down slightly to form patties. Bake for 10 minutes, flip them over, and bake for another 13 to 15 minutes or until browned on the outside and firm.

3 Make the tabouleh. Pat dry the cucumber noodles to remove moisture. Pulse the cauliflower florets in a food processor until rice-like. Add the onion, parsley, mint, salt and pepper, lemon juice, and zest to the food processor and pulse until well combined.

4 Prepare the tzatziki. Whisk the ingredients in a medium bowl.

5 Assemble the meal. Combine the cucumber noodles and the tabouleh mixture in a large bowl and toss to blend well. Divide into serving bowls and top with hot tomato balls. Drizzle over the tzatziki sauce and serve.

Cucumber Noodle Salad with Feta, Arugula, and Red Wine Vinaigrette

MAKES
2 servings

TIME TO PREPARE
15 minutes

NUTRITIONAL INFORMATION
SERVING SIZE: **2 cups**
Calories: 222
Fat: 18 g
Carbohydrates: 14 g
Sodium: 215 mg
Protein: 4 g
Sugar: 8 g

This fresh cucumber noodle salad will quickly become a favorite for every occasion. Besides looking effortlessly gorgeous, it can rise to any occasion: add some protein and make a meal out of it; serve it at a barbecue to complement grilled meats and fish; or start a meal with it to spike the palate. The cucumber noodles are crunchy and elegant, and they soak up the dressing better than greens would.

1 Make the vinaigrette. In a medium bowl, whisk the ingredients together.

2 Prepare the salad. Pat the cucumber noodles dry with paper towels to remove moisture. Transfer to a large bowl and add the arugula and onion noodles, then toss to combine.

3 Pour the vinaigrette on top, tossing to coat the vegetables. Add the feta, lightly toss, and transfer to a serving bowl or platter.

For the vinaigrette
2 tablespoons olive oil
3 tablespoons red wine vinegar
1 tablespoon lemon juice
½ teaspoon dried oregano
Salt and pepper
1 teaspoon honey

For the salad
1 large cucumber, spiralized with BLADE A
2 cups packed baby arugula
½ red onion, spiralized with BLADE C
¼ cup crumbled feta cheese

If you're making this as a full meal, spiralize half a cucumber and half a zucchini (instead of 1 full cucumber) for a heartier dish.

Italian Zucchini Pasta Salad

GF

MAKES
3 to 4 servings

TIME TO PREPARE
15 minutes

NUTRITIONAL INFORMATION
SERVING SIZE: **2 heaping cups**
Calories: 214
Fat: 16 g
Carbohydrates: 10 g
Sodium: 416 mg
Protein: 8 g
Sugar: 3 g

When Lu's mother came to New Jersey to meet my family, I threw a dinner party. I wasn't nervous about their meeting, but I was nervous about what to cook! I wanted to serve something that really reflected me, my Italian-American background, and my healthy kitchen skills. I decided on this classic pasta salad—just without the pasta. My sister's boyfriend, who typically doesn't like zucchini or anything else labeled "good for you," practically licked his plate clean.

1 Prepare the salad. Slice the zucchini halfway through and then spiralize using blade B. In a large bowl, combine the zucchini noodles with the artichoke hearts, tomatoes, provolone, salami, red onion, and black olives.

2 Make the dressing. Whisk the ingredients in a small bowl.

3 Pour the dressing over the pasta salad and toss to combine. Refrigerate for at least 15 minutes, until the dressing begins to soften the zucchini. Serve chilled.

The longer this pasta salad marinates in the refrigerator, the deeper the flavors get and the softer the zucchini becomes. If possible, let it sit overnight. Shake it up just before serving.

For the salad

2 medium zucchini

1 cup quartered artichoke hearts, drained and patted dry

6 cherry tomatoes, halved

½ cup cubed provolone cheese

¾ cup diced salami

½ small red onion, thinly sliced

⅓ cup quartered black olives

For the dressing

3 tablespoons red wine vinegar

2 tablespoons olive oil

¼ cup lemon juice

½ teaspoon dried oregano

½ teaspoon dried parsley

½ teaspoon dried basil

¼ teaspoon red pepper flakes

Salt and pepper

SANDWICHES, WRAPS & MORE

Tilapia Tostadas with Tomato-Corn Salsa

Tuna Parsnip Portobello Melts

Beet Rice Nori Rolls with Chipotle-Teriyaki Sauce

Chicken Banh Mi with Sriracha Greek Yogurt

Collard Hummus Wraps with Golden Beets and Sprouts

Spicy Shrimp Lettuce Wraps with Coconut-Lime Jícama Rice

Jalapeño Turkey Burgers with Cilantro-Lime Kohlrabi

Arugula, Olive, and Onion Sweet Potato Pizza Stacks

Apple-Potato Cheese Bun

Tilapia Tostadas with Tomato-Corn Salsa

MAKES
3 large tostadas

GF

TIME TO PREPARE
20 minutes

TIME TO COOK
25 minutes

NUTRITIONAL INFORMATION
SERVING SIZE: **1 plantain tostada with 3 ounces of tilapia**
Calories: 532
Fat: 9 g
Carbohydrates: 78 g
Sodium: 128 mg
Protein: 41 g
Sugar: 20 g

Top a traditional tostada with anything and it'll taste good—but it won't leave you feeling good. Mexican tostadas are fried corn tortillas, but this Inspiralized version is baked and is made with plantain rice. By binding the rice with coconut flakes, the mixture hardens during baking and creates a tostada base with a hint of sweetness and the right amount of crunch. The spicy tilapia pairs well with the refreshing tomato-corn salsa. This recipe will turn your taco night into plantain tostada night!

Cooking spray

1 ear of corn, shucked and silks removed

2 large medium-ripe plantains, peeled, spiralized with BLADE C, then riced (see page 25)

1 large egg and 1 egg white, lightly beaten

2 tablespoons unsweetened coconut flakes

Salt and pepper

3 (3-ounce) pieces of tilapia fillet

1 teaspoon chili powder

1 lime, cut into 3 thick slices

For the salsa

⅓ cup diced red onion

½ cup diced seeded ripe tomatoes

1 tablespoon lime juice

Salt and pepper

1 (14-ounce) can black beans, rinsed and drained

2 tablespoons water

1 tablespoon lime juice

1 tablespoon minced fresh cilantro

1 cup shredded romaine lettuce

1 tablespoon crumbled queso fresco

1 Preheat the oven to 400 degrees. Line two baking sheets with parchment paper and lightly coat with cooking spray.

2 Place the corn in a medium saucepan and cover with salted water. Bring to a boil over high heat and cook for 2 to 3 minutes or until easily pierced with a fork. When cool to the touch, slice the kernels off into a small bowl.

3 In a medium bowl, combine the plantain rice with the beaten eggs and coconut flakes. Toss to coat, and season with salt and pepper. Using your hands, place a third of the plantain mixture on one of the prepared baking sheets. Flatten and round out the edges to make it tostada shaped. Repeat with the remaining mixture, placing all three tostadas on the same baking sheet. Bake for 15 to 17 minutes, until solid.

4 Season the tilapia with the chili powder, salt, and pepper. Squeeze a lime slice over each, transfer to the remaining prepared baking sheet, and bake for 13 to 15 minutes alongside the tostadas.

5 Prepare the salsa: Mix all the ingredients in a medium bowl. Add the corn kernels.

6 Heat the beans in a small saucepan with the water and lime juice until warmed through. Transfer to a food processor, add the cilantro, and pulse until the mixture becomes pasty but still has some chunks.

7 Assemble the tostadas. Smear each tostada with the bean mixture and top with shredded lettuce. Layer on the tilapia, breaking the pieces into chunks. Add the salsa and the queso fresco, then serve immediately.

You can turn this tostada into a pliable soft taco by baking it for only 13 to 15 minutes.

Tuna Parsnip Portobello Melts

MAKES
2 melts

GF

TIME TO PREPARE
15 minutes

TIME TO COOK
25 minutes

NUTRITIONAL INFORMATION
SERVING SIZE:
1 portobello melt with
1 slice of cheese
Calories: 269
Fat: 13 g
Carbohydrates: 24 g
Sodium: 543 mg
Protein: 18 g
Sugar: 4 g

ALSO WORKS WELL WITH
Sweet Potatoes ·
Rutabaga · Potatoes

My Grandma Ida loves tuna salad with crackers. I can't even begin to count the number of times she came to my parents' house and my mother brought out the tuna with mayo and a stack of saltines. Eventually, even though Grandma Ida didn't, *I* graduated to tuna melts. Now I use "fayonnaise" to make my tuna melts with nonfat Greek yogurt, which has more zing and doesn't pack on the processed fat. These melts require a little extra time, but your taste buds will thank you. The warm portobello mushrooms and the nutty parsnip noodles are reason enough to love them—but if you need more reasons, there are also the melted provolone, a healthier tuna salad, and juicy tomatoes. These melts are best eaten with a knife and fork, since delicious can sometimes be a little messy!

For the mushrooms
- 2 large portobello mushroom caps, gills and stem end scooped out
- 1 tablespoon olive oil, plus 2 tablespoons for brushing
- 1 medium garlic clove, minced
- Pinch of red pepper flakes
- 1 large parsnip, peeled, spiralized with **BLADE C**
- Salt and pepper

For the tuna fayonnaise
- 3 tablespoons plain nonfat Greek yogurt
- 1 teaspoon Dijon mustard
- ¼ teaspoon garlic powder
- Salt and pepper
- 3 teaspoons fresh lemon juice
- 1 (5-ounce) can solid white albacore tuna in water, drained

For the melts
- 4 thin tomato slices
- 2 slices provolone cheese
- 3 teaspoons chopped chives

1 Preheat the oven to 400 degrees. Line a baking sheet with foil.

2 Prepare the mushrooms. Spread the portobello caps evenly on the baking sheet, gill side up. Brush both sides with olive oil and season with salt and pepper. Bake for 10 minutes or until slightly wilted.

3 Place a large skillet over medium heat and add the tablespoon olive oil. When the oil is shimmering, add the garlic and red pepper flakes, and cook for 30 seconds or until fragrant. Add the parsnip noodles and season with salt and pepper. Cover and cook for 5 minutes, uncovering and tossing occasionally, until the parsnip noodles are al dente. Remove from the heat.

4 Make the tuna fayonnaise. Combine the yogurt, mustard, garlic powder, salt and pepper, and lemon juice in a medium bowl. Fold in the tuna and check the seasonings.

5 Assemble the melts. Remove the baking sheet from the oven, but keep the oven on. Pat the roasted mushrooms as dry as possible. In the center of each cap place half the parsnip noodles. Top each with half the tuna mixture, then with 2 tomato slices. Place a slice of provolone on each cap and return the baking sheet to the oven to bake the mushrooms for 5 minutes more, or until the cheese is melted. Sprinkle the mushroom melts with chives and serve.

Want to barbecue these? Even better! Sear the portobello mushrooms on the grill first.

Beet Rice Nori Rolls with Chipotle-Teriyaki Sauce

MAKES
2 rolls (12 pieces)

TIME TO PREPARE
25 minutes

NUTRITIONAL INFORMATION
SERVING SIZE: 1 roll (6 pieces) + ¼ cup of dipping sauce
Calories: 290
Fat: 18 g
Carbohydrates: 32 g
Sodium: 1257 mg
Protein: 6 g
Sugar: 25 g

ALSO WORKS WELL WITH
Zucchini · Kohlrabi · Carrots

Is the answer ever *no* to the question, "Want to grab some sushi tonight?" Sushi is gorgeous and colorful, and it comes in so many different flavor combinations, but the sticky rice can pack a high calorie, sugar, and carbohydrate count, leaving you feeling heavy afterward. So ditch the pricey sushi joint and make your own, using spiralized vegetable rice! With beet rice, you're adding nutrients and color while you subtract the not-so-good-for-you stuff. That equation sounds Inspiralized to me.

1 Make the sauce. Pulse the ingredients in a food processor or high-speed blender until creamy. Season to taste.

2 Make the rolls. Working with one sheet at a time, place a nori on a clean, dry surface. Smear the avocado all over, covering completely in a thin layer. Sprinkle the beet rice evenly over, using the back of a spoon to press gently into the avocado. Place the cucumber noodles on the bottom quarter of the sheet.

3 Rolling away from your body, roll the nori and rice over the cucumber noodles, adding pressure and compressing the roll with your fingers so that it is tightly formed. Continue until nori is entirely rolled. Repeat for the second nori sheet.

4 Using a sharp knife, slice each roll into 6 pieces. Drizzle the sauce over the pieces or serve it alongside for dipping.

For the sauce
¼ cup low-sodium soy sauce

2 tablespoons honey

½ teaspoon minced fresh ginger

1 tablespoon toasted sesame oil

1 chipotle chile in adobo sauce, with 1 teaspoon sauce

1 teaspoon minced garlic

For the nori rolls
2 sheets nori (dried seaweed)

1 avocado, mashed

1 medium beet, peeled, spiralized with **BLADE D**, then riced (see page 25)

½ seedless cucumber, spiralized with **BLADE D**

It's essential that your avocado mash be completely
smooth. If this layer is too thick or chunky, the sushi
will be too difficult to roll and will fall apart.

Chicken Banh Mi with Sriracha Greek Yogurt

MAKES
4 sandwiches

TIME TO PREPARE
20 minutes

TIME TO COOK
15 minutes

NUTRITIONAL INFORMATION
SERVING SIZE: 1 sandwich
Calories: 260
Fat: 6 g
Carbohydrates: 27 g
Sodium: 595 mg
Protein: 24 g
Sugar: 23 g

ALSO WORKS WELL WITH
Zucchini · Onions

One of my simplest tricks is to eat sandwiches open-faced—not only for health reasons but also for greater flavor! If you've ever had a banh mi sandwich, you know the bun can easily overpower the delicious pickled vegetable filling in this classic Vietnamese street food. Here, I've replaced the bun with a bell pepper, which not only offers a hydrating crunch but also is a low-calorie, low-carbohydrate vehicle for showcasing what you came for: the pickled (spiralized) vegetables, Asian marinated chicken, and a high-protein Sriracha spread made with nonfat Greek yogurt.

For the pickled vegetables
¼ cup rice vinegar

2 tablespoons honey

½ teaspoon salt

1 small daikon radish, peeled, spiralized with BLADE D

1 medium carrot, peeled, spiralized with BLADE D

1 medium cucumber, spiralized with BLADE D

For the chicken
1 tablespoon extra-virgin olive oil

1 tablespoon low-sodium soy sauce

1 tablespoon hoisin sauce

1 tablespoon lime juice

1 teaspoon honey

¾ to 1 pound boneless chicken breast, cut into strips

For the Sriracha yogurt
⅓ cup plain nonfat Greek yogurt

1 tablespoon Sriracha or other hot sauce

For the sandwiches
2 large red bell peppers

⅓ cup fresh cilantro leaves

(recipe continues)

1 Pickle the vegetables. Whisk together the vinegar, honey, and salt in a medium bowl. Add the daikon radish, carrot, and cucumber noodles; toss to coat well, then marinate in the refrigerator until ready to assemble the sandwiches, tossing every 5 minutes.

2 Prepare the chicken. Whisk together the olive oil, soy sauce, hoisin sauce, lime juice, and honey in a shallow dish. Add the chicken and turn to coat. Heat a large grill pan over medium heat. When a bit of water flicked onto the pan sizzles, add the chicken and grill for 10 minutes, flipping halfway through, until no longer pink. Cut into thin slices.

3 Make the yogurt. In a small bowl, whisk the ingredients.

4 Assemble the sandwiches. Slice the tops off both peppers, remove and discard the seeds and white flesh, and halve them vertically to yield four sandwich "bottoms." Lay out the bell pepper pieces with the insides facing up. Spread on the Sriracha mayo, then layer on the chicken and top with the pickled vegetables. Drizzle the tops with extra yogurt, if desired, and garnish with the cilantro.

Collard Hummus Wraps with Golden Beets and Sprouts

MAKES
2 wraps

GF

V

P

TIME TO PREPARE
15 minutes

TIME TO COOK
10 minutes

NUTRITIONAL INFORMATION
SERVING SIZE: **1 wrap**
Calories: 225
Fat: 11 g
Carbohydrates: 28 g
Sodium: 173 mg
Protein: 7 g
Sugar: 4 g

ALSO WORKS WELL WITH
Zucchini · Cucumbers
· Carrots

Collard greens are nature's sandwich wrap. These large cabbage-family plants yield giant leaves that are perfect for holding ingredients. Here, the warm roasted golden beets practically melt into the creamy avocado and hummus, while the alfalfa sprouts add a great texture. This collard wrap is quick to make and it packs a big nutritional punch—perfect for fueling up on busy days of blogging and cooking.

1 Preheat the oven to 400 degrees. Line a baking sheet with parchment paper. Spread the beet noodles in an even layer and lightly coat with olive oil cooking spray. Season with salt and pepper. Roast for 10 minutes or until softened, tossing halfway through.

2 Lay the collard leaves on a clean, dry surface. Spread the center of each with about half the hummus, leaving a 1- to 1½-inch border.

3 Divide the beet noodles between the leaves, atop the hummus. Add 2 slices of avocado to each leaf, then top with alfalfa sprouts. Fold the sides in and roll the leaves up like a burrito. Slice each in half, and secure with toothpicks before serving.

1 large golden beet, peeled, spiralized with BLADE C

Olive oil cooking spray

Salt and pepper

2 large collard leaves, thick center stems removed as much as possible

½ cup hummus

½ avocado, quartered

1 cup alfalfa sprouts

Spicy Shrimp Lettuce Wraps with Coconut-Lime Jícama Rice

Lettuce wraps are life-changing. They are a cleaner, healthier alternative to a processed tortilla or wrap, and they are versatile. Here, we have a Latin American vibe, with the chili powder, coconut, lime, and jícama. Each lettuce wrap has a breezy Caribbean taste, perfectly suitable for noshing at the beach—or at least for closing your eyes and pretending that's where you are!.

1 Marinate the shrimp. Combine the shrimp, spices, and olive oil in a bowl and toss to coat evenly. Place in refrigerator to chill while you continue cooking.

2 Prepare the jícama rice. Heat the olive oil in a medium nonstick skillet over medium heat. When the oil is shimmering, add the garlic and onion. Cook for 2 to 3 minutes, or until the onion is translucent. Add the jícama rice, lime juice, and coconut flakes and stir to combine. Cover the skillet and cook for 5 minutes, stirring occasionally, until the jícama rice is cooked through and no longer crunchy.

3 Place a large nonstick skillet over medium heat. When a little water flicked onto the skillet sizzles, add the marinated shrimp. Cook for 2 to 3 minutes per side, until opaque and pink.

For the shrimp
8 ounces raw small shrimp, peeled and deveined
1 teaspoon chili powder
½ teaspoon smoked paprika
Salt and pepper
1 tablespoon olive oil

For the jícama rice
1 tablespoon extra-virgin olive oil
1 tablespoon minced garlic
½ white onion, sliced into thin strips
1 medium jícama, peeled, spiralized with BLADE C, then riced (see page 25) and drained
Juice of 1 lime (2 to 3 tablespoons), plus more to serve
1 tablespoon coconut flakes

8 to 10 Bibb lettuce leaves

4 Assemble the wraps. Place ⅓ to ½ cup jícama rice in the middle of a lettuce leaf and top with a shrimp. Repeat with remaining leaves, jícama rice, and shrimp. Serve immediately, with additional lime juice squeezed over, if desired.

Try trimmed jícama noodles instead of jícama rice for a different texture.

113

Jalapeño Turkey Burgers with Cilantro-Lime Kohlrabi

MAKES
4 burgers

TIME TO PREPARE
20 minutes

TIME TO COOK
15 minutes

NUTRITIONAL INFORMATION
SERVING SIZE: **1 burger and 1 cup of kohlrabi salad**
Calories: 347
Fat: 16 g
Carbohydrates: 18 g
Sodium: 56 mg
Protein: 27 g
Sugar: 8 g

ALSO WORKS WELL WITH
Jícama

Ordering a burger at a restaurant and asking to replace the bun with a side salad is an easy trick for enjoying a burger without feeling stuffed. The only problem is that the usual side salad doesn't do justice to the burger. In this version, cilantro, lime, jalapeño, and avocado go together even better than peanut butter and jelly, making this burger with salad a winning combo. The subtle touch of jalapeño in the lean turkey burgers marries well with the tangy lime zest in the crunchy kohlrabi salad. Will you ever need burger buns again? Maybe not.

For the slaw

2 celery stalks, peeled

2 medium kohlrabi, peeled, spiralized with BLADE C

4 tablespoons lime juice

Grated zest of 1 lime

¼ cup chopped fresh cilantro

1 tablespoon extra-virgin olive oil

3 teaspoons red wine vinegar

3 teaspoons honey

Salt and pepper

2 tablespoons fresh orange juice

For the burgers

2 small garlic cloves, minced

Salt and pepper

1 pound lean ground turkey

2 teaspoons minced jalapeño

1 teaspoon ground coriander

2 tablespoons chopped fresh parsley

1 firm ripe avocado, diced

1 tablespoon extra-virgin olive oil

2 ¼-inch-thick slices of beefsteak tomato

1 tablespoon fresh lime juice

1 Make the slaw. Combine the ingredients in a medium bowl. Set in the refrigerator to marinate while you prepare the burgers.

2 Make the burgers. Combine the garlic, salt and pepper, turkey, jalapeño, coriander, parsley, and avocado in a medium bowl. Using your hands, form two equal patties. Heat the olive oil in a large skillet over medium heat. When the oil is shimmering, add the burgers and cook for 3 minutes or until the bottoms are browned. Flip and cook for another 3 to 5 minutes or until the burgers are cooked through. Transfer to a serving plate.

3 Using the same skillet, over medium-high heat, add the tomato slices and season with salt and pepper and the lime juice. Cook for 1 minute, flip over, and sear another 30 seconds on the other side, until the tomatoes are warmed through.

4 Top each burger with a tomato slice and serve with the kohlrabi slaw alongside.

It's important that the avocado is not overripe—slightly firm is best for stuffing into burgers. If it's too soft, it will make the whole burger mushy.

Arugula, Olive, and Onion Sweet Potato Pizza Stacks

MAKES
6 mini-pizzas

GF

TIME TO PREPARE
30 minutes

VT

TIME TO COOK
30 minutes

NUTRITIONAL INFORMATION
SERVING SIZE: **1 mini-pizza**
Calories: 273
Fat: 20 g
Carbohydrates: 14 g
Sodium: 492 mg
Protein: 14 g
Sugar: 6 g

ALSO WORKS WELL WITH
Rutabaga · Potatoes ·
Parsnips

It's definitely possible to cook spiralized vegetables together in a skillet so that they form a pizza-like base, but it's tough to serve—the noodles tend to fall apart and the "crust" quickly becomes soggy. After a lot of experimenting, I found it easier to make mini-pizzas with a bun bottom, with each mini-pizza serving as a slice. These are great for parties, and the recipe can easily be doubled to serve twelve.

1 Preheat the oven to 450 degrees. Place a large nonstick skillet over medium heat and coat with cooking spray. When a little water flicked onto the skillet sizzles, add the sweet potato noodles and season with garlic powder, salt, and pepper. Cover and cook for 5 to 7 minutes, or until the noodles are softened and lightly browned.

2 Transfer the sweet potato noodles to a medium bowl, allow to cool for 1 to 2 minutes, then add the eggs and stir well. Fill six 6-ounce ramekins halfway with the noodles. Cover each with a piece of foil and push the foil down so that it's touching the noodles. Place a can over the foil and press firmly to compress the noodles. Refrigerate at least 15 minutes so that the noodles set.

Cooking spray

2 medium sweet potatoes, peeled, spiralized with BLADE C

1½ teaspoons garlic powder

Salt and pepper

2 large eggs, lightly beaten

3½ tablespoons olive oil

½ red onion, thinly sliced

1 large garlic clove, minced

Pinch of red pepper flakes

6 tablespoons marinara sauce

1 (8-ounce) ball or log of mozzarella cheese, thinly sliced

¾ cup halved green olives

2 tablespoons grated Parmesan cheese

2 cups packed baby arugula

(recipe continues)

3 Heat ½ tablespoon olive oil in a medium nonstick skillet over medium-high heat. When the oil is shimmering, add the onion, garlic, and red pepper flakes. Cook for 3 to 4 minutes or until the onion is wilted.

4 Heat 1 tablespoon olive oil in a large nonstick skillet over medium heat. When the oil is shimmering, add two of the buns, flipping the ramekins over the skillet and patting the ramekin bottoms until the buns fall out. Cook for 3 minutes or until the noodles set, being sure to push in any stray noodles. Carefully flip and cook, flattening with the back of the spatula, another 2 to 3 minutes or until the bun is set and browned. Repeat with the remaining buns, adding 1 tablespoon oil for each batch.

5 Line a baking sheet with foil and coat the foil with cooking spray. Arrange the sweet potato buns in a single layer and top each bun with 1 tablespoon marinara sauce and some sliced mozzarella. Season with salt and pepper and bake for 5 minutes or until the cheese melts.

6 Remove the pizzas from the oven and cover evenly with the sautéed onion, the olives, and Parmesan cheese. Top with the arugula. Bring the buns together in a round to form a "pizza," or serve individually.

You'll need six 6-ounce ramekins to make these mini-pizzas.

Apple-Potato Cheese Bun

MAKES
4 buns

GF

VT

TIME TO PREPARE
20 minutes

TIME TO COOK
15 minutes

NUTRITIONAL INFORMATION
SERVING SIZE: 1 bun
Calories: 171
Fat: 8 g
Carbohydrates: 21 g
Sodium: 38 mg
Protein: 5 g
Sugar: 4 g

ALSO WORKS WELL WITH
Sweet Potato ·
Parsnips

One of my oldest friends used to wow us with her ability to cook grilled cheese sandwiches perfectly in a skillet when we were growing up. Not many kids knew how to cook—but Dana did. We'd go to her house to paint our nails, talk about boys, and scrapbook. Afterward, we'd watch her stand confidently over the stovetop, making grilled cheeses. This Inspiralized adaptation is great for kids or for adults who want a healthier, gluten-free version of the classic sandwich.

1 large potato, peeled, spiralized with BLADE C

2 eggs, beaten

1 apple, spiralized with BLADE C

½ cup shredded Cheddar cheese
    Salt and pepper, to taste

1½ tablespoons extra-virgin olive oil

1 Place a large nonstick skillet over medium heat and coat with cooking spray. Add in the potato noodles and cover, cooking for 6 to 8 minutes, uncovering occasionally to toss, until the potato noodles start to brown, soften, and are cooked through.

2 In a large bowl, place the egg, apple, potato noodles, and cheese. Toss to combine thoroughly and season with salt and pepper.

3 Place a small skillet over medium heat and add in half of the olive oil. Once the oil shimmers, it's ready. Add in ½ cup of the apple-potato mixture and place in the center of the skillet. Cook for 2 to 3 minutes or until the bottom of the bun is fully set. Flip over carefully, press down with a spatula to compact it, and cook for another 3 to 5 minutes or until the sandwich is completely firm.

4 Repeat with the remaining mixture and the rest of the olive oil, making 4 buns. Serve immediately.

You can easily make this recipe into a casserole for serving many by spreading out the potato and apple noodles in a casserole dish, mixing them together with cheese, and then sprinkling some additional cheese on top before baking.

CASSEROLES

Mediterranean Beet and Feta Skillet Bake

Deconstructed Zucchini Manicotti

Vegetarian Carrot Enchilada Bake

Rutabaga Turkey Casserole with Gruyère-Broccoli Bread Crumbs

Vegan Chipotle Carrot Mac and Cheese

Parsnip and Kale Gratin

Stuffed Grape Leaves Casserole

Fennel Sausage and Butternut Squash Casserole

Chicken and Broccoli Skillet Bake

Mediterranean Beet and Feta Skillet Bake

MAKES
4 to 6 servings

TIME TO PREPARE
20 minutes

TIME TO COOK
25 minutes

NUTRITIONAL INFORMATION
SERVING SIZE: ½ cup with
¼ cup of feta
Calories: 148
Fat: 11 g
Carbohydrates: 8 g
Sodium: 459 mg
Protein: 6 g
Sugar: 5 g

When Lu and I went on our first vacation together to Greece, everywhere we stopped we ordered a Greek salad and a regional beer. We quickly learned that the American version of this vegetarian salad was different from the real thing, which is lettuce free and has predominantly thick-cut tomatoes with large chunks of feta. Here, I use the traditional salad mix for a hot dish. The combination of olives, onions, and fresh tomatoes is heavenly—the beet noodles only enhance all that flavor!

1 Preheat the oven to 400 degrees. In a large bowl, combine all the ingredients except the cheese and the parsley for garnish.

2 Place the block of feta or halloumi in the center of a large oven-safe skillet. Top and surround it with the beet noodle mixture. Cover with foil and bake for 20 minutes or until the beet noodles wilt. Serve hot, garnished with the remaining parsley.

Serve this with pita chips and celery sticks as a dipping appetizer, or enjoy it as a heartier main course topped with chickpeas, grilled shrimp, or chicken.

½ cup halved yellow cherry tomatoes

½ cup halved red cherry tomatoes

2 medium garlic cloves, minced

2 tablespoons chopped fresh parsley, plus 1 teaspoon for garnish

1 teaspoon dried oregano

3 teaspoons red wine vinegar

½ cup pitted Kalamata olives

1 tablespoon extra-virgin olive oil

2 small beets, peeled, spiralized with BLADE C

½ small red onion, peeled, spiralized with BLADE C

Salt and pepper

1 (8-ounce) block of feta or halloumi cheese

Deconstructed Zucchini Manicotti

MAKES
2 servings

GF

VT

TIME TO PREPARE
10 minutes

TIME TO COOK
40 minutes

NUTRITIONAL INFORMATION
SERVING SIZE: **Half the skillet (3 cups)**
Calories: 577
Fat: 26 g
Carbohydrates: 63 g
Sodium: 1258 mg
Protein: 33 g
Sugar: 6 g

When I make dinner, I'm usually cooking for one or two, but that's not to say I don't love a beef lasagna or a cheesy baked ziti. This manicotti skillet was born of necessity: I was desperately craving manicotti, but I didn't want to buy all of the ingredients and have a ton of leftovers. So I made a skillet version just for Lu and me: two mounds of manicotti filling nestled in zucchini noodles, easy for sharing. The zucchini noodles make the dish much lighter, fresher, and frankly, more fun to eat. Without the starchy pasta you more appreciate the decadent filling, which is where most of the flavor is anyway.

1 Preheat the oven to 375 degrees.

2 Place a large cast iron or nonstick skillet over medium heat and add the olive oil. When the oil is shimmering, add the garlic, red pepper flakes, and onion, and cook for 2 to 3 minutes or until the onion is translucent. Add the tomatoes and their juices, season with salt and pepper, and stir. Increase the heat to medium-high and bring to a boil, then lower to a simmer. After 5 minutes, add the basil. Continue to simmer the sauce for 5 minutes more or until it is thickened.

3 Make the filling. Combine the cheeses and egg in a large bowl. Season with salt and pepper.

For the sauce
½ tablespoon olive oil
1 large garlic clove, minced
   Pinch of red pepper flakes
½ cup diced red onion
1 (14.5-ounce) can diced tomatoes, no salt added
   Salt and pepper
5 basil leaves, chopped

For the filling
¼ cup grated Parmesan cheese
1 scant cup ricotta cheese
¼ cup shredded mozzarella cheese
1 small egg
   Salt and pepper
   Cooking spray
3 cups baby spinach

2 zucchini, spiralized with BLADE A
2 tablespoons shredded mozzarella cheese, for topping

(recipe continues)

4 Place a medium nonstick skillet over medium heat and coat with cooking spray. When some water flicked onto the skillet sizzles, add the spinach and toss until wilted, about 2 minutes. Remove from the heat and fold into the cheese mixture.

5 Assemble the manicotti. Reserve half the sauce and spread the remaining evenly on the bottom of the skillet. Place the zucchini noodles on top, then add the remaining sauce. Create two wells in the noodles and add the cheese filling. Sprinkle the mozzarella over the skillet and season with pepper. Cover with foil and bake for 20 to 25 minutes or until the noodles have softened and the cheese is melted. Serve hot.

If you want to make this skillet dish into a true casserole, double or triple the recipe to make either four or six pockets for the filling.

Vegetarian Carrot Enchilada Bake

MAKES
4 to 6 servings

GF
VT

TIME TO PREPARE
25 minutes

TIME TO COOK
35 minutes

NUTRITIONAL INFORMATION
SERVING SIZE:
1¹/₂ heaping cups
Calories: 360
Fat: 15 g
Carbohydrates: 37 g
Sodium: 280 mg
Protein: 16 g
Sugar: 7 g

ALSO WORKS WELL WITH
Butternut Squash ·
Rutabaga · Golden
Beets · Sweet
Potatoes

Basically, this recipe is a big vegetarian enchilada dish without the tortillas. Let's do the math: subtracting the tortillas leaves us with the beans, corn, vegetables, and spices. Instead of preparing a flour-based enchilada sauce, we use canned tomatoes and extra spices. *Plus* we have irresistible melted cheese on top. By removing the traditional starchy element, it's a much lighter yet still filling version of enchiladas.

Cooking spray

2 ears of corn, shucked and silks removed

1 tablespoon olive oil

1 teaspoon minced garlic

¾ cup diced white onion

1 cup diced red bell pepper

1 (14-ounce) can black beans, drained and rinsed

1 jalapeño, finely chopped

2 teaspoons ground cumin

2 teaspoons dried Mexican oregano

3 teaspoons chili powder

2 tablespoons chopped fresh cilantro

Salt and pepper

1 tablespoon fresh lime juice

1 (14-ounce) can crushed tomatoes

3 large carrots, peeled, spiralized with BLADE C, then riced (see page 25)

1 cup shredded sharp Cheddar cheese

½ cup shredded pepper jack cheese

½ cup black olives

(recipe continues)

1 Preheat the oven to 375 degrees. Coat a 4-quart casserole dish with cooking spray.

2 Place the corn in a medium saucepan, cover with salted water, and bring to a boil over high heat. Cook for 2 minutes or until the corn turns bright yellow and is easily pierced with a fork. Set aside to cool.

3 Heat the olive oil in a large pot over medium heat. When the oil is shimmering, add the garlic, onion, and bell pepper. Cook for 2 to 3 minutes or until the onion is translucent. Add the beans, jalapeño, cumin, oregano, chili powder, and cilantro. Slice the corn kernels into the pot with a knife, then season with salt, pepper, and lime juice. Toss to combine and cook for 2 to 3 minutes, until the flavors set. Add the tomatoes and carrot rice and cook for about 2 minutes to warm through. Transfer the mixture to the prepared casserole dish.

4 Combine the cheeses in a small bowl, then sprinkle over the casserole. Cover with foil and bake for 15 minutes, until the carrot rice is cooked through. Uncover and bake for 5 to 10 minutes more or until the cheese is melted and begins to bubble. Serve warm, topped with the black olives.

This dish saves well for leftovers, so make a portion without the cheese and store it in the refrigerator in an airtight container. In the morning you can top it with a fried egg for a flavorful breakfast. Yum!

Rutabaga Turkey Casserole with Gruyère-Broccoli Bread Crumbs

MAKES
3 to 6 servings

GF

TIME TO PREPARE
20 minutes

TIME TO COOK
45 minutes

NUTRITIONAL INFORMATION
SERVING SIZE: **2 cups**
Calories: 344
Fat: 15 g
Carbohydrates: 7 g
Sodium: 146 mg
Protein: 35 g
Sugar: 4 g

Rutabaga noodles work well in casseroles because they're resilient and they absorb flavors well. Rutabaga is less starchy than other root vegetables, and when it roasts, it becomes sweet *and* savory at once. The melted Gruyère adds elegant flavor and ensures that every bite is gooey and delectable. Top it all off with broccoli bread crumbs to add a fluffy texture.

1 Preheat the oven to 400 degrees. Place a large saucepan over medium heat and add the olive oil. When the oil is shimmering, add the garlic, red pepper flakes, and onion. Cook 2 to 3 minutes or until the onion is translucent. Push the mixture to the edges of the skillet and add the turkey to the center. Season with oregano, salt, and pepper. Cook, breaking up the meat as it cooks, for 3 to 5 minutes, or until browned. Stir to combine the ingredients in the pan.

2 Add the rutabaga noodles and toss to combine. Cook for 5 minutes or until the noodles begin to soften. Transfer to a 4-quart casserole dish.

3 Pulse the broccoli florets in a food processor until they take on a chunky, crumb-like consistency. In a medium bowl, combine the broccoli and the Gruyère, and season with salt and pepper. Evenly sprinkle the mixture over the casserole. Cover with foil and bake for 30 minutes or until the cheese is melted and the rutabaga noodles are cooked through. Cut into portions and serve warm.

1 tablespoon olive oil

1 large garlic clove, minced
   Pinch of red pepper flakes

½ white onion, thinly sliced

1 pound lean ground turkey

1 teaspoon dried oregano
   Salt and pepper

1 medium rutabaga, peeled, spiralized
   with BLADE C

1 cup broccoli florets

1 cup shredded Gruyère cheese

Waxy white potatoes offer a saltier flavor and can be easily substituted in here.

Vegan Chipotle Carrot Mac and Cheese

MAKES
4 to 6 servings

GF

TIME TO PREPARE
30 minutes

V

TIME TO COOK
25 minutes

NUTRITIONAL INFORMATION
SERVING SIZE: 1 cup
Calories: 267
Fat: 18 g
Carbohydrates: 19 g
Sodium: 531 mg
Protein: 9 g
Sugar: 6 g

ALSO WORKS WELL WITH
Sweet Potatoes ·
Beets · Butternut
Squash · Zucchini ·
Rutabaga

This dish is the ultimate guilt-free mac and cheese recipe: pastaless and cheeseless! How does that work, you ask? While the cashews provide thickness, the nutritional yeast adds that cheesy flavor. The natural sugar in the carrots is released as this casserole bakes, making for an exquisite, sweet bite with a special chipotle kick. Don't ask any more questions—just make this recipe and enjoy it.

1 Preheat the oven to 350 degrees. Coat a 9 x 12-inch casserole dish with cooking spray.

2 Heat the olive oil in a nonstick skillet over medium-low heat. When the oil is shimmering, add the onion and garlic. Season with salt and pepper and cook for 2 to 3 minutes or until the onion is translucent. In a blender, combine the cooked onion and garlic, the cashews, broth, chiles, and nutritional yeast. Season with salt and pepper and continue to blend until creamy, about 1 minute.

3 Slice the carrots halfway through lengthwise, then spiralize using blade B. Place the noodles in the casserole dish and top with the cashew mixture. Cover with foil and bake for 20 minutes or until the carrot noodles are cooked through. Uncover and cook 5 minutes more or until lightly golden brown on top.

Cooking spray
1 tablespoon olive oil
½ cup diced white onion
3 medium garlic cloves, minced
Salt and pepper
1 cup raw cashews
1½ cups vegetable broth
2 chipotle chiles in adobo sauce, finely chopped
2 tablespoons nutritional yeast flakes
2 large carrots, peeled

Don't have time for a casserole? Simply cook the carrot noodles in a saucepan or boil in water for 2 minutes, then add the heated sauce for a quicker meal.

Parsnip and Kale Gratin

MAKES
4 to 6 servings

GF

VT

TIME TO PREPARE
20 minutes

TIME TO COOK
1 hour 20 minutes

NUTRITIONAL INFORMATION
SERVING SIZE: **2 cups**
Calories: 391
Fat: 20 g
Carbohydrates: 36 g
Sodium: 435 mg
Protein: 19 g
Sugar: 5 g

ALSO WORKS WELL WITH
Potatoes · Sweet
Potatoes · Rutabagas
· Beets · Butternut
Squash

If truth be told, I never understood the purpose of a gratin until I made my own, using parsnips instead of potatoes. Since parsnips are slightly sweet and nutty, they taste amazing with melted Gouda on top. Kale and garlic add texture while infusing the dish with nutrition. Although the parsnips look like potatoes in this gratin, they add extra nutrients and they lower the overall carbohydrate and calorie count. If you're looking for something to make or bring for a winter dinner or holiday party, try this gratin—the parsnips can be our little secret!

1 Preheat the oven to 425 degrees. Coat a 6 x 9-inch baking dish with cooking spray. Slice the parsnips halfway lengthwise, being careful not to cut farther down than the center. Spiralize using blade A.

2 Heat the olive oil in a large skillet over medium heat. When the oil is shimmering, add the garlic and red pepper flakes, and cook for 30 seconds or until fragrant. Add the kale and 2 teaspoons of the thyme, and season with salt and pepper. Sauté for 3 to 5 minutes or until the kale is cooked through and wilted.

3 Layer one-fourth of the parsnip noodles into the baking dish and top with one-third of the kale. Top with another one-fourth of the parsnip noodles, then 1 cup of the Gouda, and season with ¼ teaspoon thyme. Add the kale again, then the parsnip noodles, then another cup of Gouda, and the remaining ¼ teaspoon thyme. Repeat once more, ending with the Gouda. Cover with foil and bake for 25 to 30 minutes or until the noodles are al dente.

Cooking spray
4 large parsnips, peeled
1 tablespoon olive oil
2 medium garlic cloves, minced
¼ teaspoon red pepper flakes
6 packed cups chopped fresh kale leaves
2½ teaspoons fresh thyme
Salt and pepper
3 cups shredded Gouda cheese

Stuffed Grape Leaves Casserole

MAKES
4 to 6 servings

GF

TIME TO PREPARE
30 minutes

V

TIME TO COOK
35 minutes

P

NUTRITIONAL INFORMATION
SERVING SIZE: **1 heaping
cup**
Calories: 161
Carbohydrates: 17 g
Sodium: 232 mg
Protein: 3 g
Sugar: 10 g

ALSO WORKS WELL WITH
Golden Beets ·
Rutabaga · Turnips

After a few failed attempts at stuffing grape leaves at home, I almost gave up—but I then decided to try them as a casserole. As it turns out, the grape leaves work better this way: you get even more stuffing in every bite. Serve slices of this alongside a fresh salad with halloumi cheese and Kalamata olives, and you'll be transported straight to the Mediterranean.

1 Preheat the oven to 350 degrees. Coat a 2-quart baking dish with cooking spray.

2 Fill a medium saucepan with water and bring to a boil over high heat. When the water is boiling, add the grape leaves. Cook for 1 minute to blanch, then drain and pat dry.

3 Heat 1 tablespoon olive oil in a large nonstick skillet over medium heat. When the oil is shimmering, add the garlic and cook for 30 seconds or until fragrant. Add the celeriac rice and toss, then add the broth and tomato. Generously season with salt and pepper and cook for 3 to 5 minutes, stirring occasionally, until the liquid has evaporated.

4 Transfer the mixture to a large bowl. Add the lemon juice, herbs, currants, and pine nuts. Stir to combine.

Cooking spray

1 (8-ounce) jar brined grape leaves (or 25 to 30 fresh leaves)

2 tablespoons olive oil

4 medium garlic cloves, minced

2 celeriac knobs, peeled, spiralized with BLADE C, then riced (see page 25)

1½ cups vegetable broth

½ cup seeded and chopped ripe tomato

Salt and pepper

½ cup lemon juice

4 tablespoons chopped fresh dill

5 tablespoons chopped fresh parsley

3 tablespoons chopped fresh mint

½ cup dried currants or dark raisins

½ cup pine nuts

5 Line the bottom and the sides of the casserole dish with the grape leaves, overlapping and allowing them to hang over the sides. Spread the rice mixture in an even layer over the grape leaves. Top with another layer of grape leaves. Fold the overhanging grape leaves together, rolling them down into the casserole and pinching tightly together to secure. Brush the top with the remaining 1 tablespoon olive oil and bake for 25 to 30 minutes or until the tops of the leaves darken and the casserole is firm.

Fennel Sausage and Butternut Squash Casserole

MAKES
4 to 6 servings

GF

TIME TO PREPARE
20 minutes

TIME TO COOK
40 minutes

NUTRITIONAL INFORMATION
SERVING SIZE: **2 heaping cups**
Calories: 573
Fat: 37 g
Carbohydrates: 43 g
Sodium: 959 mg
Protein: 21 g
Sugar: 13 g

ALSO WORKS WELL WITH
Sweet Potatoes ·
Rutabaga · Celeriac

When you combine seasonal ingredients at their peak, you get one super-flavorful dish. Case in point: this casserole unites winter fennel with winter squash. The anise taste and the squash sweetness are truly symbiotic. And to top it all off, there's the rich, salty pecorino romano cheese. Escape the cold and enjoy the winter with this warm, inviting casserole.

1 Preheat the oven to 375 degrees. Coat a 9 x 13-inch casserole dish with cooking spray.

2 Heat the olive oil in a large saucepan over medium heat. When the oil is shimmering, add the sausage meat and onion. Cook for 5 minutes or until the sausage is browned. Add the red pepper flakes and garlic, and cook for 30 seconds or until the garlic is fragrant. Then add the tomatoes, cheese, walnuts, and parsley. Stir in the butternut squash rice. Season with salt and pepper, and toss to combine.

3 Transfer the mixture to the prepared casserole dish and spread evenly. Bake for 25 to 30 minutes or until the squash rice is softened and cooked through. Serve immediately.

Cooking spray

1 tablespoon olive oil

5 pork sausages with fennel, casings removed and meat crumbled

1 medium red onion, diced

½ teaspoon red pepper flakes

3 medium garlic cloves, minced

1 (14.5-ounce) can diced tomatoes, with juice

½ cup grated pecorino romano cheese

1 cup rough-chopped walnuts

3 tablespoons minced fresh parsley

1 large butternut squash, peeled, spiralized with BLADE C, then riced (4 cups rice; see page 25)

Salt and pepper

Chicken and Broccoli Skillet Bake

MAKES
4 to 6 servings

TIME TO PREPARE
20 minutes

TIME TO COOK
40 minutes

NUTRITIONAL INFORMATION
SERVING SIZE: **2 cups**
Calories: 428
Fat: 25 g
Carbohydrates: 6 g
Sodium: 349 mg
Protein: 45 g
Sugar: 2 g

This chicken and broccoli casserole is the best of both worlds. By replacing the traditional pasta with broccoli, you still have the al dente consistency of pasta but gain more nutrients and flavor. If your broccoli stems yield more half-moons than noodles, don't fret. The melted Havarti and Cheddar will pull everything together.

1 Preheat the oven to 400 degrees. Place an oven-safe 12-inch skillet over medium heat and add 1 tablespoon olive oil. When the oil is shimmering, add the chicken, season with salt and pepper, and cook for 3 minutes per side or until lightly browned. Transfer to a plate along with any juices.

2 Bring a medium saucepan of salted water to a boil. Add the broccoli florets and noodles and cook until the florets are tender, 2 to 3 minutes. Drain.

3 Using the skillet from the chicken, heat the remaining 2 tablespoons olive oil over medium-high heat. When the oil is shimmering, add the garlic and onion, and cook for 2 to 3 minutes or until the onion is translucent. Whisk in the chicken broth and stir until the mixture thickens, about 2 minutes. Season with the thyme, parsley, and onion powder. Add the cooked chicken and the broccoli noodles and florets, and toss to combine. Top evenly with the cheeses.

4 Cover with foil and bake for 25 minutes or until bubbling. Remove the foil and broil for another 3 to 5 minutes or until the top turns golden brown.

3 tablespoons extra-virgin olive oil
1 pound boneless chicken breast, diced
　Salt and pepper
2 large broccoli heads, florets removed, stems spiralized with **BLADE D**
2 medium garlic cloves, minced
½ cup diced white onion
½ cup chicken broth
¼ teaspoon dried thyme
¼ teaspoon dried parsley
¼ teaspoon onion powder
1 cup shredded sharp Cheddar cheese
½ cup shredded Havarti cheese

To add even more flavor and texture to this casserole, toss in 1 cup spiralized sweet potato rice before baking.

RICE DISHES

Beet Superfood Bowl

Short Ribs with Sweet Potato "Grits"

Mustard and Herb-Crusted Rack of Lamb with "Couscous"

Teriyaki Salmon Balls with Ginger-Pineapple Rice

Pork Bibimbap with Ginger Gochugaru

Sweet Potato Fried Rice

Spicy Seafood-Chorizo Paella

Jícama-Stuffed Peppers with Asiago

Vegetarian Chana Masala with Kohlrabi

Beet Superfood Bowl

MAKES
3 to 4 servings

GF

V

TIME TO PREPARE
15 minutes

TIME TO COOK
15 minutes

NUTRITIONAL INFORMATION
SERVING SIZE:
1½–2 heaping cups
Calories: 312
Fat: 14 g
Carbohydrates: 38 g
Sodium: 178 mg
Protein: 12 g
Sugar: 14 g

You've probably heard the word *superfood* used a million times before, but what does it actually mean? Superfoods are low in calories and high in nutrients. What happens when you eat several superfoods in one dish? Your skin will glow, you'll rev up your metabolism, and you'll boost your immune system. I often make this dish when I need a burst of energy and nutrients before a grueling travel schedule.

1 Rinse the quinoa and place in a small saucepan with the water. Bring to a boil over high heat, then lower the heat and simmer for 15 minutes or until the quinoa is fluffy. If the quinoa is not yet fluffy, add ¼ cup water and continue to cook, repeating as necessary until fluffy.

2 In a large bowl, combine the beet rice, spinach, almonds, avocado, and edamame.

3 In a small bowl, whisk together the dressing ingredients.

4 Add the quinoa to the beet rice mixture, pour the dressing on top, and toss. Serve immediately.

½ cup uncooked quinoa

1½ cups water

2 medium beets, peeled, spiralized with BLADE C, then riced (see page 25)

2 cups packed fresh spinach

⅓ cup slivered almonds

1 avocado, cubed

1 cup cooked edamame

For the dressing

¼ cup apple cider vinegar

2 tablespoons lime juice

1 tablespoon chopped fresh mint

2 tablespoons honey

Salt and pepper

Short Ribs with Sweet Potato "Grits"

MAKES
2 to 3 servings

TIME TO PREPARE
15 minutes

TIME TO COOK
2 hours 30 minutes

NUTRITIONAL INFORMATION
SERVING SIZE: ¼ **pound boneless short ribs and ½ cup of grits**
Calories: 527
Fat: 34 g
Carbohydrates: 26 g
Sodium: 914 mg
Protein: 29 g
Sugar: 10 g

ALSO WORKS WELL WITH
Rutabaga · Carrots

I never thought about applying to colleges in the South—until I tagged along on a road trip to North Carolina with my mom to drop off my sister at camp. Tired from all the driving, we snuggled into a local restaurant in Davidson and asked the waitress to bring us "something Southern." What did we get? A big bowl of grits. I didn't like their bland taste and couldn't even get a full spoonful down, but a few years later, during my freshman year at Wake Forest University (also in North Carolina), I decided to give them a second try. I ordered shrimp and grits for dinner, and they were wonderful because they were cheese grits! Whether you prefer your grits simple or with cheese, at breakfast, lunch, or dinner, you'll love this version, using sweet potato rice instead of hominy grits, paired with melt-in-your-mouth short ribs.

For the short ribs
1 pound boneless short ribs
Salt and pepper
1 tablespoon olive oil
1 cup diced white onion
1 cup diced celery
2 medium garlic cloves, minced
¾ cup hearty red wine (such as Chianti)
3 cups canned crushed tomatoes
1½ cups low-sodium beef broth

For the cheese "grits"
1 tablespoon olive oil
1 medium garlic clove, minced
1 large sweet potato, peeled, spiralized with BLADE C, then riced (see page 25)
Salt and pepper
1 cup low-sodium beef broth
4 teaspoons minced fresh parsley
½ cup shredded sharp Cheddar cheese

1 Make the short ribs. Preheat the oven to 350 degrees. Season the short ribs generously with salt and pepper. Heat the olive oil in a large Dutch oven or oven-safe pot over medium-high heat. When the oil is shimmering, add the short ribs, being sure not to crowd the pan. Brown for 3 to 4 minutes per side, then transfer to a plate.

2 Reduce the heat to medium-low. Add the onion, celery, and garlic and cook for 2 to 3 minutes or until the onion is translucent. Add the wine, tomatoes, and broth, and season again with salt and pepper. Increase the heat to high and bring to a boil, then reduce to low and add the short ribs. Cover and transfer to the oven to cook for about 2½ hours or until the meat is very tender.

3 Make the cheese "grits." Heat 1 tablespoon olive oil in a large pot over medium heat. When the oil is shimmering, add the garlic and cook for 30 seconds or until fragrant. Add the sweet potato rice, season with salt and pepper, and stir. Cook for 2 minutes to heat through, then add the broth. Turn the heat to low and simmer for 10 to 15 minutes or until the broth is evaporated. Stir in 3 teaspoons of the parsley, then remove the pot from the heat and fold in the cheese. Stir until the cheese has melted.

4 Spoon the sweet potato rice into bowls and top with the short ribs and a spoonful of juices from the pot. Sprinkle with the remaining 1 teaspoon parsley and serve hot.

For more of a corn taste, add ½ cup pureed cooked corn to the sweet potato rice mixture.

Mustard and Herb-Crusted Rack of Lamb with "Couscous"

MAKES
4 servings

TIME TO PREPARE
25 minutes

TIME TO COOK
30 minutes

NUTRITIONAL INFORMATION
SERVING SIZE: **2 ribs
+ 1 cup of couscous**
Calories: 437
Fat: 30 g
Carbohydrates: 25 g
Sodium: 752 mg
Protein: 20 g
Sugar: 12 g

ALSO WORKS WELL WITH
Sweet Potatoes ·
Carrots · Beets ·
Kohlrabi

Cooking a rack of lamb can be intimidating, but this recipe is much easier than it looks. It could become your go-to meal for guests. The meat is well seasoned and the flavor and consistency of the turnip rice are unique, so it's sure to be a hit. The turnip rice fluffs up as it simmers in the vegetable broth, creating a couscous-like texture with the deep flavor suitable for accompanying such an impressive meat.

For the bread crumbs
- 1 slice whole wheat bread, torn into pieces
- 1 medium garlic clove, chopped
- 1 tablespoon chopped fresh thyme leaves
- 1 tablespoon chopped fresh rosemary leaves
- 1 teaspoon chopped fresh parsley

For the lamb
- 1 rack of lamb (8 ribs)
- Salt and pepper
- 1 tablespoon olive oil
- 1 to 1½ tablespoons whole-grain or country-style Dijon mustard

For the turnip rice
- 1 yellow bell pepper, stem removed
- 1 tablespoon olive oil
- 1 large garlic clove, minced
- 1 medium red onion, thinly sliced
- 5 celery stalks, finely diced
- 4 large turnips, peeled, spiralized with BLADE C, then riced (see page 25)
- Salt and pepper
- ¾ cup low-sodium chicken broth
- Chopped fresh parsley, for garnish

(recipe continues)

1 Preheat the oven to 400 degrees. Line a baking sheet with parchment paper.

2 Prepare the bread crumbs. Combine the ingredients in a food processor and pulse until crumb-like.

3 Roast the lamb. Season the rack with salt and pepper. Place a large grill pan or cast iron skillet over medium heat and add the olive oil. When the oil is shimmering, add the lamb, fat side down, and sear for 1 to 2 minutes. Flip and cook for 1 additional minute to lightly sear on the other side. Remove from the heat and spread the mustard over the fat side of the rack. Sprinkle the bread crumbs over the mustard and gently press down to fully adhere. Transfer to the prepared baking sheet and roast for 20 to 25 minutes or until cooked to your liking.

4 Make the turnip rice. Place the bell pepper directly over the stovetop flame and char it all over, turning occasionally, until the skin is almost completely blackened, about 10 minutes. (If you do not have a gas stove, heat the broiler and line a baking sheet with tin foil. Slice off the top of the bell pepper and remove the seeds. Slice the pepper in half and lay skin-side up on the foil. Set the sheet 5 inches away from the heat source and broil for 5 to 10 minutes or until peppers are blackened all over.) Transfer to an airtight container to cool.

5 Place a large nonstick skillet over medium heat and add the olive oil. When the oil is shimmering, add the garlic, onion, and celery; cook for 2 to 3 minutes or until the onion is translucent. Add the turnip rice and season with salt and pepper. Pour in the chicken broth and cook for 5 to 7 minutes or until the turnip rice begins to brown slightly.

6 Remove the pepper from the container and peel off the charred skin. Halve the pepper, then remove and discard the seeds. Slice lengthwise into strips. Add the roasted pepper to the turnip rice.

7 Remove the lamb from the oven and allow it to rest on a cutting board for 5 minutes. Divide the couscous among four plates. Carve the rack of lamb into eight individual ribs and place two ribs on top of each plate of turnip rice. Garnish with parsley and serve.

Teriyaki Salmon Balls with Ginger-Pineapple Rice

MAKES
3 servings

TIME TO PREPARE
20 minutes

TIME TO COOK
20 minutes

NUTRITIONAL INFORMATION
SERVING SIZE:
3 meatballs +
1 heaping cup of rice
Calories: 336
Fat: 13 g
Carbohydrates: 28 g
Sodium: 952 mg
Protein: 28 g
Sugar: 16 g

ALSO WORKS WELL WITH
Sweet Potatoes ·
Beets · Kohlrabi

These salmon balls happened accidentally. I was making dinner for Lu and me, but realized I had only one small salmon fillet. Since the rest of the recipe was already prepped, I started to make salmon burgers, but I had no bread crumbs. Staring into my fridge, I spotted a few broccoli florets and had the idea to turn *them* into bread crumbs. The result? Perfectly soft salmon balls with a subtle hint of warm broccoli! I'll never make them any other way again!

For the teriyaki sauce
- ¼ cup low-sodium soy sauce
- 1 medium garlic clove, minced
- 1 teaspoon grated fresh ginger
- 1 tablespoon honey
- 2 tablespoons mirin
- Pepper

For the salmon balls
- ½ cup broccoli florets
- 1 (10-ounce) salmon fillet, skin removed
- 2 tablespoons minced shallots
- 2 teaspoons minced garlic
- Salt and pepper

For the rice
- 1 tablespoon virgin coconut oil
- 1 teaspoon minced fresh ginger
- 1 teaspoon minced garlic
- ½ cup chopped scallions, green and white parts
- 2 large carrots, peeled, spiralized with BLADE C, then riced (see page 25)
- 1 cup diced pineapple
- Salt and pepper

(recipe continues)

1 Preheat the oven to 400 degrees. Line a baking sheet with parchment paper.

2 Make the teriyaki sauce. Whisk the ingredients in a small bowl and set aside.

3 Make the salmon balls. Place the broccoli florets in a food processor and pulse until the consistency of bread crumbs. Add the salmon, shallots, garlic, and salt and pepper. Pulse until the salmon breaks into small pieces and the broccoli crumbs are evenly dispersed. Using your hands, form the mixture into nine 1-inch balls and place on the prepared baking sheet. Bake for 11 to 13 minutes, flipping halfway through.

4 Brush the salmon balls with some of the teriyaki sauce. Return the salmon balls to the oven and bake for 5 minutes more.

5 Prepare the rice. Place a large nonstick skillet over medium heat and add the coconut oil. When the oil is shimmering, add the ginger, garlic, and scallions. Cook until fragrant, about 30 seconds, then add the carrot rice, pineapple chunks, and 1 tablespoon teriyaki sauce. Season with salt and pepper and toss to combine. Cook for 5 to 7 minutes or until slightly softened.

6 Divide the rice into portions and top each with three salmon balls.

These salmon balls pair well with zucchini noodles sautéed with ginger, garlic, and sesame oil.

Pork Bibimbap with Ginger Gochugaru

MAKES
2 servings

TIME TO PREPARE
20 minutes

TIME TO COOK
15 minutes

NUTRITIONAL INFORMATION
SERVING SIZE: **3 cups**
Calories: 489
Fat: 28 g
Carbohydrates: 23 g
Sodium: 455 mg
Protein: 38 g
Sugar: 12 g

ALSO WORKS WELL WITH
Zucchini · Carrots ·
Turnips

Everything tastes better with a fried egg on top! Bibimbap is a Korean dish of rice and mixed vegetables. Before you dig in, though, you're supposed to stir the ingredients together to unify it. What makes it unified? The egg! When the yolk breaks, it coats the ingredients and marries for a complex bite loaded with flavor. But the daikon radish here becomes the star of this rice bowl once it's cooked with the ginger, garlic, scallions, and gochugaru.

1½ tablespoons virgin coconut oil or vegetable oil

8 ounces lean ground pork

2 teaspoons low-sodium soy sauce

1½ tablespoons minced garlic

Salt and pepper

1 teaspoon minced fresh ginger

½ cup diced scallions, green and white parts

2 large daikon radishes, peeled, spiralized with BLADE D, then riced (see page 25) and drained

½ teaspoon gochugaru

½ tablespoon toasted sesame oil

2 packed cups fresh spinach

Cooking spray

2 large eggs

½ teaspoon white sesame seeds

1 medium cucumber, spiralized with BLADE C and patted dry

(recipe continues)

1 Place a large nonstick skillet over medium heat and add ½ tablespoon coconut oil. When the oil is shimmering, add the pork and cook, breaking it up with a wooden spoon. Add the soy sauce and 1 tablespoon garlic, and season with salt and pepper. Cook for about 5 minutes or until the pork is browned. Transfer to a bowl and cover.

2 In the same skillet, over medium heat, add the remaining 1 tablespoon coconut oil. When the oil is shimmering, add the ginger and remaining ½ teaspoon garlic and cook for 30 seconds or until fragrant. Stir in the scallions and daikon rice. Cook for 1 minute or until the rice begins to turn light brown, then sprinkle on the gochugaru. Stir to combine and cook for about 5 minutes to heat the daikon rice through, stirring frequently. Transfer to a bowl and cover.

3 In the same skillet, heat the sesame oil over medium heat. When the oil is shimmering, add the spinach and cook until wilted, tossing frequently, about 2 minutes. Transfer to a plate.

4 Return the skillet to medium heat and coat with cooking spray. Crack in the eggs and cook without stirring for 3 to 5 minutes or until the egg whites are set and the yolks are still runny.

5 Evenly divide the daikon rice, pork, spinach, and cucumber noodles between two bowls. Sprinkle the sesame seeds over the spinach. Top each bowl with a fried egg and serve immediately.

A Korean chile powder made from dried gochu chiles, gochugaru can be difficult to find in some grocery stores. If you don't have an Asian market near you, you can order it online. There's no proper substitute, and you'll love this dish so much that I promise you'll use the gochugaru again.

Sweet Potato Fried Rice

MAKES
2 cups rice

GF

VT

P

TIME TO PREPARE
10 minutes

TIME TO COOK
10 minutes

NUTRITIONAL INFORMATION
SERVING SIZE: **1 cup**
Calories: 236
Carbohydrates: 22 g
Sodium: 239 mg
Protein: 10 g
Sugar: 7 g

ALSO WORKS WELL WITH
Carrots · Beets ·
Kohlrabi · Turnips ·
Daikon Radish ·
Butternut Squash

When I first started spiralizing, I tried to re-create all my favorite carb dishes, and fried rice was number one on my list. Introduce me to someone who doesn't love fried rice, because I'd love to meet that person. It's a takeout classic! This Inspiralized version mimics the original and tastes even better when chilled as leftovers—just like the real deal!

1 Heat the oil in a large nonstick skillet over medium heat. When the oil is shimmering, add the onion and cook for 2 minutes or until translucent. Add the sweet potato rice and the broth, season with salt and pepper, and cook for 1 minute, stirring frequently to warm the sweet potato rice. Reduce the heat and simmer, allowing the liquid to evaporate, about 5 minutes. If the rice is still crunchy, stir and cook for another 2 minutes.

2 Heat a medium nonstick skillet over medium heat. When a bit of water flicked onto the skillet sizzles, add the eggs and briefly scramble them.

3 Fold the scrambled eggs and the peas into the sweet potato rice mixture. Add the soy sauce and toss to combine. Serve hot.

1 tablespoon vegetable, olive, or coconut oil

½ medium white onion, diced

1 large sweet potato, peeled, spiralized with BLADE C, then riced (see page 25)

½ cup low-sodium vegetable or chicken broth

Salt and pepper

2 large eggs, lightly beaten

½ cup cooked frozen or fresh green peas

1 teaspoon low-sodium soy sauce

For a stickier fried rice, omit the broth and double the oil. This way, the rice will take longer to soften and will brown along the way.

Spicy Seafood-Chorizo Paella

MAKES
4 to 5 servings

GF

P

TIME TO PREPARE
20 minutes

TIME TO COOK
25 minutes

NUTRITIONAL INFORMATION
SERVING SIZE: **2 cups**
Calories: 158
Fat: 4 g
Carbohydrates: 17 g
Sodium: 307 mg
Protein: 13 g
Sugar: 7 g

ALSO WORKS WELL WITH
Kohlrabi · Butternut
Squash · Beets

When I studied abroad, I dreamed about visiting Barcelona. I wasn't dreaming of gorgeous people in high fashion, the outstanding architecture, the striking scenery, or a rich history and culture. No, I was dreaming of paella—big skillets of it filled with meats, seafood, and Spanish seasonings. Once there, every paella, whether a tapas portion or dinner size, left me awestruck. This paella is a healthier, simplified version of one of the world's truly memorable dishes.

1 Heat the olive oil in a large skillet over medium heat. When the oil is shimmering, add the garlic, red pepper flakes, onion, and bell pepper. Cook for 2 to 3 minutes or until vegetables soften. Add the chorizo and cook for 2 to 3 minutes or until it begins to brown. Add the tomatoes, peas, carrot rice, chili powder, paprika, turmeric, lemon juice, cilantro, salt, and pepper. Stir to combine.

2 Press the cod and shrimp into the rice. Cover the skillet and allow the mixture to cook undisturbed for 5 to 7 minutes or until the seafood is cooked through. Garnish with parsley and serve immediately.

If you have a paella pan, use it. If not, the largest, deepest skillet you have will do just fine.

1 tablespoon olive oil

1 tablespoon minced garlic

¼ teaspoon red pepper flakes

½ cup diced yellow onion

1 small green bell pepper, diced

1 large chorizo sausage, thinly sliced (about ¼ inch)

1 (14.5-ounce) can diced tomatoes

½ cup frozen peas

2 large carrots, peeled, spiralized with BLADE C, then riced (see page 25)

1 teaspoon chili powder

1 teaspoon smoked paprika

½ teaspoon ground turmeric

2 tablespoons lemon juice

1 tablespoon chopped fresh cilantro
    Salt and pepper

4 ounces cod fillet, chopped into 1-inch cubes

12 medium shrimp, defrosted if frozen, peeled and deveined

2 teaspoons minced fresh parsley

Jícama-Stuffed Peppers with Asiago

MAKES
6 to 8 pepper halves

GF

VT

TIME TO PREPARE
15 minutes

TIME TO COOK
40 minutes

NUTRITIONAL INFORMATION
SERVING SIZE: **1 pepper half**
Calories: 120
Fat: 9 g
Carbohydrates: 6 g
Sodium: 252 mg
Protein: 4 g
Sugar: 1 g

ALSO WORKS WELL WITH
Celeriac · Turnips ·
Butternut Squash ·
Sweet Potatoes

One of the first things I ever cooked for myself was quinoa-stuffed peppers, using a recipe from *Vegetarian Times*. That dish inspired this one. It seems super fancy, but it's easy to make. I love anything I can pop in the oven and serve without having to worry about plating—it looks gorgeous on its own. When you slice into these poblano peppers, the cilantro and lightly spiced jícama rice transport you to Mexico, but with an Italian twist added by the salty Asiago cheese.

1 Preheat the oven to 375 degrees. Coat a rimmed baking sheet or shallow casserole dish with cooking spray.

2 Heat the olive oil in a large saucepan over medium heat. When the oil is shimmering, add the garlic and onion. Cook for 2 minutes or until the onion is translucent.

3 Add the avocado, cilantro, olives, jícama rice, oregano, cumin, and chili powder. Season with salt and pepper and stir to combine. Cook for 2 to 3 minutes to allow the jícama rice to fully absorb the flavors and take on the colors of the seasonings.

4 Transfer the mixture to a large bowl, add half the cheese, and toss well.

Cooking spray

½ tablespoon olive oil

2 teaspoons minced garlic

½ cup diced red onion

1 avocado, cubed

1 tablespoon chopped fresh cilantro

½ cup quartered black olives

1 small jícama, peeled, spiralized with BLADE C, then riced (see page 25) and drained

½ teaspoon dried Mexican oregano

¼ teaspoon ground cumin

1 teaspoon chili powder

Salt and pepper

1 cup shredded Asiago cheese

4 large poblano peppers

(recipe continues)

5 Slice off and discard the tops of the peppers, halve them lengthwise, and discard the seeds and any white flesh. Stuff the pepper halves with as much jícama rice mixture as possible, and place on the baking sheet. Sprinkle the remaining Asiago over the stuffed peppers.

6 Cover the peppers with foil and bake for 20 minutes. Remove the foil and continue baking for 5 minutes more or until the cheese is bubbling and beginning to brown on top. Serve hot.

Make the Spicy Jícama Strings (page 56) and save some leftovers for this recipe. Throw them into a food processor, pulse until rice-like, and add them to the stuffing mixture. This trick will save you time *and* add more spice to the peppers.

Vegetarian Chana Masala with Kohlrabi

MAKES
4 servings

GF

VT

TIME TO PREPARE
15 minutes

TIME TO COOK
30 minutes

NUTRITIONAL INFORMATION
SERVING SIZE: 1/2 cup rice + 1/2 cup chana marsala
Calories: 457
Fat: 9 g
Carbohydrates: 67 g
Sodium: 555 mg
Protein: 21 g
Sugar: 13 g

ALSO WORKS WELL WITH
Carrots · Celeriac ·
Butternut Squash ·
Beets · Sweet
Potatoes

The beauty of using spiralized vegetables is that they add freshness and lightness to even the heaviest of dishes, such as this South Indian chickpea curry. The flavors are deep, aromatic, and thick, while the kohlrabi is crisp and deliciously refreshing.

1 tablespoon virgin coconut oil

1 white onion, diced

3 large garlic cloves, minced

1 tablespoon minced fresh ginger

1 serrano chile, seeded and minced

1½ teaspoons garam masala

1½ teaspoons ground coriander

2 teaspoons ground cumin

½ teaspoon ground turmeric

¼ teaspoon cayenne pepper

Salt

1 (28-ounce) can crushed tomatoes

1 tablespoon fresh lemon juice

2 (14-ounce) cans chickpeas, drained and rinsed

2 large kohlrabi, peeled, spiralized with BLADE C, then riced (see page 25)

⅓ cup plain nonfat Greek yogurt

1½ tablespoons chopped fresh cilantro

(recipe continues)

1 In a large saucepan, heat the oil over medium heat. When the oil is shimmering, add the onion, garlic, ginger, and chile. Cook for about 3 minutes or until the onion turns translucent. Add the garam masala, coriander, cumin, turmeric, and cayenne. Season with salt and cook for 2 more minutes or until the vegetables absorb the spices. Add the tomatoes and lemon juice, increase the heat to high, bring to a boil, and add the chickpeas. Then reduce the heat to low and simmer for 10 to 15 minutes to let the flavors develop.

2 Place a large nonstick skillet over medium heat. When a little water flicked onto the skillet sizzles, add the kohlrabi rice. Cook for 3 to 5 minutes, stirring frequently or until softened and warmed through. Remove the pan from heat and set aside.

3 Stir the yogurt and cilantro into the chickpeas. Serve in bowls alongside the kohlrabi rice.

To make use of the thick kohlrabi greens, chop them up and add about 3 cups to the simmering curry.

PASTAS & NOODLES

Beet Pasta with Blood Orange, Honey Walnuts, and Crispy Kale

Sesame Almond Butter Kohlrabi Bowl

Bacon Cacio e Pepe

Pesto Spaghetti with Heirloom Grape Tomatoes

Spicy Garlic Crab with Parsnips

Zucchini Linguine with Garlic Clam Sauce

Halibut en Papillote with Butternut Squash

Bikini Bolognese

Albondigas and Chayote with Tomato-Serrano Sauce

Thai Drunken Zucchini Noodles with Pork

Vegan Celeriac Alfredo with Broccolini

Sweet Potato Carbonara

Seared Ahi Tuna with Chimichurri

Pesto Turnips with Shredded Brussels Sprouts

Tofu Miso-Tahini Carrot Bowl

Beet Pasta with Blood Orange, Honey Walnuts, and Crispy Kale

MAKES
2 servings

TIME TO PREPARE
15 minutes

TIME TO COOK
20 minutes

NUTRITIONAL INFORMATION
SERVING SIZE:
**2 cups salad
+ 2.5 tablespoons
dressing**
Calories: 383
Fat: 26 g
Carbohydrates: 33 g
Sodium: 155 mg
Protein: 7 g
Sugar: 15 g

ALSO WORKS WELL WITH
Golden Beets ·
Butternut Squash

When you're a food blogger, you are especially aware of produce seasonality. You know it's fall when your Twitter feed is full of pumpkin everything—lattes, cookies, pancakes, smoothies, granola, you name it. One day, I signed on to learn that blood oranges were in season and I had almost missed out on them! I rushed to the grocery store, picked up a few, and headed back to the kitchen to make a recipe before my small window of relevancy closed. I was happy I did—when you roast an orange, it somehow transforms into a velvety, luxurious, and sweetened version of itself.

For the vinaigrette

Juice from ¼ large lemon

Salt and pepper

1 tablespoon olive oil

1 tablespoon water

2 teaspoons red wine vinegar

¼ cup orange juice

1 teaspoon whole-grain or country-style Dijon mustard

For the salad

2 medium beets, peeled, spiralized with BLADE C

Olive oil

Salt and pepper

Cooking spray

1 large blood orange, peeled and quartered or cut into eighths

2 cups roughly chopped kale leaves (stems removed)

½ cup walnuts

Raw honey

You can always buy kale chips instead of roasting your own, but if you have the time, make them fresh and save the leftovers for snacking.

(recipe continues)

1 Make the vinaigrette. Whisk the ingredients in a small bowl and refrigerate.

2 Prepare the salad. Preheat the oven to 375 degrees. Place the beet noodles on a baking sheet and drizzle lightly with olive oil. Season with salt and pepper and roast in the oven for 15 minutes.

3 Lightly coat a separate baking sheet with cooking spray and place the orange pieces on one side and the kale on the other. Lightly coat the kale with the cooking spray and season with salt and pepper. Bake for 10 to 12 minutes, then transfer the kale to a platter.

4 Add the walnuts where the kale was. Drizzle lightly with honey and toss carefully with tongs. Return the baking sheet to the oven for 5 minutes more or until the nuts are lightly toasted.

5 Divide the roasted beet noodles among serving plates and top with the orange pieces, walnuts, and kale. Drizzle the vinaigrette over and serve.

Sesame Almond Butter Kohlrabi Bowl

MAKES
3 servings

TIME TO PREPARE
15 minutes

TIME TO COOK
15 minutes

NUTRITIONAL INFORMATION
SERVING SIZE: 2 cups
Calories: 410
Fat: 31 g
Carbohydrates: 23 g
Sodium: 592 mg
Protein: 15 g
Sugar: 11 g

ALSO WORKS WELL WITH
Zucchini · Cucumbers

This dish is a spin on peanut noodles. Almond butter is higher in micronutrients, such as calcium, iron, magnesium, and vitamin E. The real kicker, though, is the kohlrabi noodles, which refresh every bite with their light taste and crunchy skin. The longer the kohlrabi sits in the dressing, the more infused it will become with flavor, so pop this dish in the refrigerator and enjoy it later.

1 Combine the almond butter, soy sauce, honey, sesame oil, lime juice, water, and salt and pepper in a food processor and pulse until creamy. Transfer to a bowl.

2 Rinse the food processor and wipe dry. Add the almonds and pulse until chunky ground, taking care not to grind into a powder.

3 Place the kohlrabi noodles in a medium bowl with the scallions. Add the almond butter sauce and the ground almonds, and toss to combine thoroughly. Top with the sesame seeds. Chill in the refrigerator or serve immediately.

½ cup smooth almond butter

3 tablespoons low-sodium soy sauce

1 tablespoon honey

1 teaspoon toasted sesame oil

1 tablespoon lime juice

1 tablespoon water

Salt and pepper

¼ cup slivered almonds (or blanched sliced almonds)

2 kohlrabi, spiralized with BLADE B

¾ cup chopped scallions, green and white parts

2 teaspoons white sesame seeds

Bacon Cacio e Pepe

MAKES
2 servings

TIME TO PREPARE
10 minutes

TIME TO COOK
15 minutes

NUTRITIONAL INFORMATION
SERVING SIZE: **2 heaping cups**
Calories: 161
Fat: 9 g
Carbohydrates: 6 g
Sodium: 360 mg
Protein: 9 g
Sugar: 3 g

ALSO WORKS WELL WITH
Parsnips · Chayote · Broccoli · Butternut Squash · Kohlrabi

Simple, sexy, and decadent, this dish has the cheeses melting together perfectly with the warmed zucchini noodles and meshing with the bacon and pepper for a taste so creamy and light you'll find it hard to believe you're not eating pasta. Most important, you can enjoy your romantic evening without feeling bloated. Ladies, if you have a hard time convincing your man to eat zucchini noodles, make him this dish—he'll be a believer after that first bite!

1 Heat a large skillet over medium heat and coat lightly with cooking spray. When a bit of water flicked onto the skillet sizzles, add the bacon and cook until crisp. Drain the bacon on a paper towel–lined plate.

2 Add the garlic and red pepper flakes to the skillet, still over medium heat, and cook for 30 seconds or until fragrant. Add the zucchini noodles and cook, tossing, for 2 to 3 minutes or until the zucchini noodles are al dente. Generously season with pepper and add the cheeses, tossing to combine thoroughly until the noodles are coated with cheese.

3 Divide between two bowls, topping each serving with more pepper and Parmigiano cheese, as desired. Crumble the bacon on top and serve.

Cooking spray

3 bacon strips

1 large garlic clove, minced

Pinch of red pepper flakes

2 medium zucchini, spiralized with BLADE C

Cracked black peppercorns

¼ cup grated pecorino romano cheese

¼ cup grated Parmigiano-Reggiano cheese, plus more for garnish

To make your zucchini noodles look more like pasta noodles, peel off the vegetable's green skin before you spiralize, as in this picture.

Pesto Spaghetti with Heirloom Grape Tomatoes

MAKES
3 servings

TIME TO PREPARE
20 minutes

NUTRITIONAL INFORMATION
**SERVING SIZE: 1½ to
2 heaping cups**
Calories: 277
Fats: 26 g
Carbohydrates: 8 g
Sodium: 113 mg
Protein: 6 g
Sugar: 4 g

ALSO WORKS WELL WITH
Beets · Kohlrabi

Next to a simple pomodoro, pesto is the quintessential pasta sauce. Its classic Italian taste can bring any pasta to life. Here, paired with zucchini noodles, it showcases the power of vegetable noodles. You're suddenly at a trattoria in Italy yet maintaining that slim waistline! If you have hesitated to start with the spiralizer, I recommend trying this recipe—it's simple, quick to make, and will absolutely please your taste buds.

1 Combine the basil, pine nuts, olive oil, salt and pepper, garlic, and Parmesan in a food processor and pulse until creamy.

2 Place the zucchini noodles and tomatoes in a large bowl, pour the pesto on top, and toss to combine. Serve.

If you prefer this dish hot, heat the zucchini noodles in a large skillet over medium heat for 2 to 3 minutes. When they are al dente, add the tomatoes and pesto, and toss for another 1 to 2 minutes, until heated through.

3 cups fresh basil leaves

3 tablespoons pine nuts

¼ cup olive oil

½ teaspoon freshly ground sea salt

¼ teaspoon freshly ground black pepper

1 large garlic clove, minced

3 tablespoons grated Parmesan cheese

2 medium zucchini, spiralized with **BLADE C**

¾ cup mixed heirloom cherry tomatoes

Spicy Garlic Crab with Parsnips

MAKES
2 servings

TIME TO PREPARE
15 minutes

TIME TO COOK
15 minutes

NUTRITIONAL INFORMATION
SERVING SIZE: **2 cups**
Calories: 312
Fat: 14 g
Carbohydrates: 27 g
Sodium: 399 mg
Protein: 22 g
Sugar: 7 g

ALSO WORKS WELL WITH
Zucchini · Chayote ·
Daikon Radish ·
Kohlrabi

While all the recipes in this cookbook are irresistibly delicious, I really mean it about this one. Parsnips are one of those vegetables that sometimes invoke a "meh" or "blah" feeling; they're usually just mashed or roasted in a medley with other root vegetables. When I started spiralizing them, though, I learned to love parsnips in a whole new way. In this dish, their sweetness works fabulously with the crab, which is prized for its own delicate, sweet taste. Now, see if you also won't be able to put your fork down.

1 Heat the olive oil in a large skillet over medium heat. When the oil is shimmering, add the garlic and red pepper flakes and cook for 30 seconds or until fragrant.

2 Add the parsnip noodles and season generously with salt and pepper. Cover and cook for 1 to 3 minutes or until the parsnip noodles are softened but still al dente, uncovering and tossing occasionally.

3 Add the crab and lemon juice, and cook for 2 minutes more or until the parsnips are cooked through and the crab is warmed. Serve hot, garnished with parsley and pea shoots.

2 tablespoons olive oil

2 medium garlic cloves, minced

¼ teaspoon red pepper flakes

2 large parsnips, peeled, spiralized with BLADE C

Salt and pepper

1 cup jumbo lump crabmeat

1 tablespoon fresh lemon juice

Minced fresh parsley

½ cup pea shoots

The gentle flavor of true crab is what elevates this recipe; imitation won't work nearly as well. While premium jumbo lump crab is best, regular lump will also do the trick.

If you're not wheat-free, serve this dish with crusty warmed whole-grain or Italian bread to sop up the sauce.

Zucchini Linguine with Garlic Clam Sauce

MAKES
3 to 4 servings

GF

P

TIME TO PREPARE
20 minutes

TIME TO COOK
25 minutes

NUTRITIONAL INFORMATION
SERVING SIZE: **about ¼ pound of clams + 1 heaping cup of pasta**
Calories: 237
Fat: 8 g
Carbohydrates: 20 g
Sodium: 1077 mg
Protein: 20 g
Sugar: 4 g

ALSO WORKS WELL WITH
Kohlrabi · Butternut Squash · Parsnips · Rutabaga · Celeriac

My favorite pasta meal growing up was my mother's garlic crab spaghetti. The ingredients were so modest, yet the flavors so vivid. As I got older and started eating out on my own, I discovered clam sauce. Clams have that same light seafood taste, but also have a more intense seafood flavor, which is absorbed by the zucchini noodles in this dish. The garlic clam sauce is wonderful on a hot summer night when you're surrounded by friends and loved ones—it will bring everyone back to the basics.

1 Place a large saucepan over medium heat and add the olive oil. When the oil is shimmering, add the garlic and shallots. Cook for 2 to 3 minutes or until shallots are translucent. Add the red pepper flakes, reserved clam juice, and wine, and season with salt and pepper. Increase the heat to high, bring to a boil, then reduce the heat to low. Simmer until the sauce is reduced by about half.

2 Add the fresh clams to the sauce and cover. Steam for 7 to 10 minutes. Discard any that don't open after 10 minutes, then add the chopped clams. Stir in the zucchini noodles and 1 tablespoon of the parsley. Cook for 2 to 3 minutes or until the zucchini noodles are al dente.

3 Divide the pasta among bowls and garnish with the remaining tablespoon parsley, the pepper, and the lemon wedges.

2 tablespoons olive oil

2 garlic cloves, minced

2 medium shallots, minced

Pinch of red pepper flakes

1 (14-ounce) can chopped clams, drained, with half the juice reserved

½ cup dry white wine (such as Sauvignon Blanc)

Salt and pepper

1½ pounds littleneck clams, rinsed and scrubbed

3 large zucchini, spiralized with BLADE C

2 tablespoons finely chopped fresh parsley

Freshly cracked black peppercorns

2 lemons, quartered

Halibut en Papillote with Butternut Squash

MAKES
4 servings

GF

P

TIME TO PREPARE
20 minutes

TIME TO COOK
15 minutes

NUTRITIONAL INFORMATION
SERVING SIZE: **1 cup of
pasta and 4 ounces
halibut steak**
Calories: 323
Fats: 13 g
Carbohydrates: 22 g
Sodium: 207
Protein: 30 g
Sugar: 3 g

One of the first meals I ever made for Lu was a fish *en papillote,* or in parchment—a preparation that sounds really fancy and complex, but is the exact opposite. It's impressive nonetheless (that's why I made it!). The juices from the halibut seep into the butternut squash noodles and steam them, locking in the flavor. When you open your parchment pouch, the aromatics are elegant and everything is cooked to perfection.

1 Preheat the oven to 400 degrees. In a large bowl, toss together the butternut squash noodles, olive oil, leek, garlic, and olives. Season with pepper.

2 Lay out four large pieces of parchment paper, about 10 x 10 inches. In the center of each, place some of the squash noodle mixture. Top with a halibut piece and drizzle each with 1 tablespoon lemon juice. Add 2 thyme sprigs to each bundle and season with salt and pepper.

3 Seal the parchment packets by crimping the edges together to make a pouch, folding over once. Place on the baking sheet and bake for 10 to 13 minutes. Place the packets on plates, slit open, and serve.

1 small butternut squash, peeled and bulbous end removed, spiralized with **BLADE C**

2 tablespoons olive oil

1 cup thinly sliced leek

2 medium garlic cloves, thinly sliced

½ cup halved green olives

　Black pepper

4 (4-ounce) pieces of halibut fillet, skin removed

¼ cup fresh lemon juice

8 fresh thyme sprigs

　Salt and pepper

All spiralized vegetables bake well in parchment except for cucumber noodles (they're too wet).

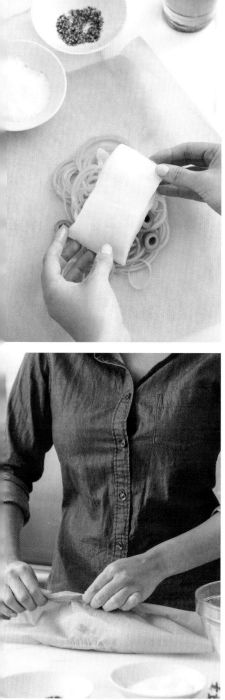

Bikini Bolognese

MAKES
2 servings

GF

TIME TO PREPARE
20 minutes

TIME TO COOK
25 minutes

NUTRITIONAL INFORMATION
SERVING SIZE:
1 heaping cup
Calories: 285
Fat: 11 g
Carbohydrates: 31 g
Sodium: 452 mg
Protein: 21 g
Sugar: 6 g

ALSO WORKS WELL WITH
Kohlrabi · Sweet
Potatoes · Carrots ·
Beets · Butternut
Squash · Rutabaga ·
Celeriac · Chayote

I'd like to think I live life with no regrets, but there might be one exception. When my family and I arrived in Rome on a vacation together, after a long day of traveling, my father used room service to order his favorite pasta dish: rigatoni and bolognese. I wasn't eating meat at the time, so I just watched as my entire family dove in. To this day I remember that giant ceramic bowl of thick rigatoni and how the aroma filled the room. Clearly, I wasn't following the "when in Rome" mantra. This recipe is an Italian classic and belongs in your arsenal.

1 Place the celery and carrot in a food processor and pulse until finely chopped; the mixture should be somewhere between chunky and pureed.

2 In a large skillet, heat the olive oil over medium heat and season with salt and pepper. When the oil is shimmering, add the garlic and cook for 30 seconds or until fragrant. Add the red pepper flakes and cook for 30 seconds. Then add the onion and cook for 1 to 2 minutes or until it begins to soften.

3 Add the carrot and celery mixture to the skillet and cook for about 2 minutes or until it begins to soften. Push the veggie mixture to one side of the pan and add the turkey, breaking it up with a wooden spoon. Add a pinch of the oregano and cook until the turkey is browned. Then combine the vegetables with the turkey in the pan and season with another pinch of oregano.

½ **celery stalk, diced**

½ **medium carrot, diced**

2 **tablespoons olive oil**

 Salt and pepper

2 **medium garlic cloves, minced**

1 **teaspoon red pepper flakes**

½ **medium red onion, chopped**

8 **ounces ground turkey**

1 **tablespoon dried oregano**

¼ **cup low-sodium chicken broth**

1 **(14.5-ounce) can crushed tomatoes (such as San Marzano)**

3 **teaspoons tomato paste**

⅓ **cup chopped fresh basil**

2 to 2½ **large zucchini, spiralized with BLADE C**

 Shavings of Parmesan cheese

4 Add the chicken broth and simmer until absorbed. Add the tomatoes and tomato paste, and season generously with salt and pepper. Sprinkle in the remaining oregano. Increase the heat to high and bring to a boil, then reduce the heat and simmer for 15 minutes.

5 Add the basil to the sauce and then add the zucchini noodles, mixing thoroughly and cooking for 2 to 3 minutes or until the zucchini noodles are al dente. Serve hot, sprinkled with Parmesan cheese.

If you like your bolognese extra-spicy, add more red pepper flakes in step 2.

Albondigas and Chayote with Tomato-Serrano Sauce

MAKES
4 servings

GF

P

TIME TO PREPARE
25 minutes

TIME TO COOK
30 minutes

NUTRITIONAL INFORMATION
SERVING SIZE: **2 cups of pasta with 2 meatballs**
Calories: 346
Fat: 11 g
Carbohydrates: 35 g
Sodium: 412 mg
Protein: 31 g
Sugar: 19 g

ALSO WORKS WELL WITH
Zucchini · Turnips ·
Rutabaga · Kohlrabi ·
Celeriac · Sweet
Potatoes · Carrots

I've taken some of my favorite flavors and created a Latin-themed meatball (*albondiga*) dish, presented here with chayote noodles. It's an adaptation of my grandparents' traditional Italian dish, altered to fit a healthier lifestyle without sacrificing flavor.

For the albondigas
- 1 pound lean ground beef
- ¼ cup diced yellow onion
- 1 large garlic clove, minced
- 1 teaspoon dried Mexican oregano
- 2½ tablespoons chopped fresh mint
- Salt and pepper

For the sauce
- 1 tablespoon olive oil
- 1 medium garlic clove, minced
- ½ cup diced yellow onion
- 2 serrano chiles, stems and seeds removed, diced
- 1 (28-ounce) can diced tomatoes
- Salt and pepper
- 2 tablespoons chopped fresh cilantro
- 3 chayotes, spiralized with BLADE C

(recipe continues)

1 Make the albondigas. Preheat the oven to 375 degrees. Line a baking sheet with parchment paper. Combine the ingredients for the albondigas in a large bowl. Using your hands, form 8 to 10 meatballs about 1 inch in diameter and space them evenly on the baking sheet. Bake for 18 to 20 minutes or until browned, flipping them halfway through.

2 Prepare the sauce. Add the olive oil to a large saucepan or pot over medium heat. When the oil is shimmering, add the garlic and cook for 30 seconds or until fragrant. Add the onion and chile, and cook for 2 to 3 minutes or until the onion is translucent. Add the tomatoes, season with salt and pepper, and crush the tomatoes using a potato masher or the back of a fork. Increase the heat to high and bring to a boil. Add the cilantro, reduce the heat to low, and simmer for 10 to 15 minutes or until the sauce thickens, stirring occasionally.

3 Add the meatballs to the sauce and continue to simmer, turning to coat them, for 1 to 2 minutes. Scoop out the meatballs and set aside, then add the chayote noodles to the sauce. Toss to combine thoroughly and cook for 3 minutes or until chayote noodles are al dente.

4 Serve the noodles warm, topped with the meatballs, and with any extra sauce spooned over.

Thai Drunken Zucchini Noodles with Pork

MAKES
2 servings

TIME TO PREPARE
15 minutes

TIME TO COOK
20 minutes

NUTRITIONAL INFORMATION
SERVING SIZE: **2 heaping cups**
Calories: 383
Fat: 22 g
Carbohydrates: 18 g
Sodium: 1387 mg
Protein: 27 g
Sugar: 10 g

Family and friends often ask me, "Are you ever stumped for recipe ideas?" I usually feel the opposite: I never know which recipes to try first because my "to make" list is pages long! But I also like to create the noodle classics—lo mein, spaghetti alfredo, and so on. I've finally created a version of Thai drunken noodles that uses flat zucchini noodles instead of wide rice noodles and has no added sugars.

1 Heat a large nonstick skillet over medium heat. When a bit of water flicked onto the skillet sizzles, add the hoisin sauce, soy sauce, oyster sauce, chili oil, and fish sauce. When the sauces have heated and combined for about 2 minutes, transfer to a bowl.

2 Add the coconut oil to the same skillet over medium heat. When the oil is shimmering, add the pork and sauté, breaking up with a wooden spoon, for 5 minutes or until cooked through and browned. Add the shallots and garlic and cook 2 to 3 minutes more or until the shallots begin to brown.

3 Return the sauce mixture to the skillet and add the bell pepper and scallions. Cook for 1 minute, stirring frequently. Add the zucchini noodles and cook 2 to 3 minutes or until the zucchini noodles soften. Fold in the Thai basil leaves and serve.

1 tablespoon hoisin sauce

1 tablespoon low-sodium soy sauce

½ tablespoon oyster sauce

1 tablespoon Thai chili oil

1 tablespoon Thai or Vietnamese fish sauce

1 tablespoon virgin coconut oil

8 ounces ground pork

2 small shallots, minced

1 medium garlic clove, minced

1 small red bell pepper, sliced into strips

2 thinly sliced scallions, green and white parts

2 medium zucchini, spiralized with **BLADE A**

3 tablespoons chopped fresh Thai basil leaves

Drunken noodles are meant to be spicy, so if you can't find Thai chili oil, use Sriracha or a chili garlic sauce.

Vegan Celeriac Alfredo with Broccolini

MAKES
4 servings

GF

TIME TO PREPARE
20 minutes

V

TIME TO COOK
20 minutes

P

NUTRITIONAL INFORMATION
SERVING SIZE: **1½–
2 heaping cups**
Calories: 155
Fat: 7 g
Carbohydrates: 19 g
Sodium: 572 mg
Protein: 7 g
Sugar: 6 g

ALSO WORKS WELL WITH
Rutabaga · Zucchini ·
Sweet Potatoes ·
Butternut Squash ·
Kohlrabi · Turnips ·
Parsnips

This vegan alfredo has a go-to sauce that works with any vegetable pasta. In this version, the earthy taste of the celeriac noodles, the warm tenderness of the broccolini, and the alfredo consistency from the cauliflower encapsulate everything *Inspiralized* is about: eating nutritious and energizing food. You'll feel like you're in Italy, twisting forkfuls of a creamy bowl of indulgence.

1 Place the cauliflower florets in a large pot and cover with salted water. Bring to a boil over high heat, then lower the heat to medium and cook for 5 to 7 minutes or until easily pierced with a fork. Remove the cauliflower with a slotted spoon.

2 With the water still boiling, add the broccolini and cook for 2 minutes or until firm-tender. Fill a medium bowl with ice cubes. Drain the broccolini and immediately place in the ice water to stop the cooking. Pat dry and then slice off the florets. Chop the stems into 1-inch pieces.

Florets from 1 small to medium cauliflower

2 bunches broccolini, about 1 inch of tough stems trimmed

2 tablespoons olive oil

2 medium garlic cloves, minced

2 tablespoons minced shallots

2 cups vegetable broth

1½ tablespoons nutritional yeast

½ teaspoon Dijon mustard

4 teaspoons fresh lemon juice

Salt and pepper

Pinch of red pepper flakes

2 large celeriac knobs, peeled, spiralized with BLADE C

2 tablespoons minced fresh parsley

(recipe continues)

3 Heat 1 tablespoon of the olive oil in a medium nonstick skillet over medium heat. When the oil is shimmering, add one garlic clove and cook for 30 seconds or until fragrant. Add the shallots and cook for 2 to 3 minutes or until translucent. Transfer to a high-speed blender or large food processor, and add the cauliflower, the vegetable broth, nutritional yeast, mustard, and lemon juice. Generously season with salt and pepper and blend the sauce until creamy, about 1 minute.

4 Return the broccolini pot to medium heat and add the remaining 1 tablespoon olive oil. When the oil is shimmering, add the remaining garlic and the red pepper flakes. Cook for 30 seconds or until fragrant, then add the broccolini florets and stems. Add the celeriac noodles. Season generously with salt and pepper, cover, and cook for 5 to 7 minutes, tossing occasionally, until the celeriac noodles are al dente. Transfer the celeriac noodles and vegetables to a serving bowl.

5 Place a medium skillet over medium-low heat and add the cauliflower sauce. Simmer to heat through, at least 5 minutes. Stir in the parsley, then pour the sauce over the noodles. Toss to combine and serve warm.

It's essential to lightly boil the broccolini first to minimize its bitterness. A quick blanch will highlight its robust, grassy, and slightly sweet flavor.

Sweet Potato Carbonara

MAKES
4 servings

GF

TIME TO PREPARE
15 minutes

TIME TO COOK
15 minutes

NUTRITIONAL INFORMATION
SERVING SIZE: 1$\frac{1}{2}$–
2 heaping cups
Calories: 345
Fat: 22 g
Carbohydrates: 21 g
Sodium: 725 mg
Protein: 14 g
Sugar: 9 g

The sweet potato noodles work well in this dish because they soak up the egg and really transform this carbonara sauce with their natural sugars. The pancetta adds savory balance. Consider this pasta a slightly sweeter, more colorful, and cleaner version of the original.

Cooking spray

2 large sweet potatoes, peeled, spiralized with BLADE C

2 tablespoons olive oil

2 medium garlic cloves, minced

¼ teaspoon red pepper flakes

½ medium red onion, diced

1 cup diced pancetta

2 large eggs

½ cup grated Parmesan cheese
   Salt and pepper

1 Heat a large nonstick skillet over medium heat and coat with cooking spray. When some water flicked onto the skillet sizzles, add the sweet potato noodles and cook for 5 to 7 minutes, tossing frequently, until softened and lightly browned.

2 Heat the olive oil over medium heat in a separate large nonstick skillet. When the oil is shimmering, add the garlic and red pepper flakes. Cook for 30 seconds, stirring frequently, until fragrant, then add the onion. Cook for 2 to 3 minutes or until the onion begins to soften. Add the pancetta, stirring frequently until cooked through, about 5 minutes more.

3 Whisk together the eggs and cheese in a medium bowl until smooth. Season with the salt and pepper.

4 Add the sweet potato noodles to the skillet with the pancetta, toss to combine, then turn off the heat. Slowly pour the egg-cheese mixture over the noodles, stirring constantly to cook the eggs and coat the noodles. Serve hot.

If you can't find pancetta at your grocery store, you can substitute bacon.

If you don't like your tuna rare, cook it for an extra 2 to 3 minutes on each side.

Seared Ahi Tuna with Chimichurri

MAKES
2 servings

GF

P

TIME TO PREPARE
20 minutes

TIME TO COOK
10 minutes

NUTRITIONAL INFORMATION
SERVING SIZE: 1 ahi tuna steak + 1 cup of pasta with chimichurri drizzle
Calories: 360
Fat: 22 g
Carbohydrates: 14 g
Sodium: 57 mg
Protein: 27 g
Sugar: 3 g

My friend Jen, who studied at Le Cordon Bleu in Paris, was in a cooking competition on television and had to make just one dish to wow the judges. When she was preparing for the show, she invited me for a recipe testing. One of the options was a dish elegantly drizzled with a chimichurri sauce. I never forgot the freshness of it and I set out to duplicate it in my own way. Here, it works wonders on these light cucumber noodles and quick-seared tuna.

1 Combine all the chimichurri ingredients in a food processor and pulse until creamy.

2 Season the fillets generously with salt and pepper on both sides, pressing to adhere. Heat the olive oil in a large nonstick skillet over medium heat. When the oil is shimmering, add the tuna and cook for 1 to 1½ minutes per side, adding the lime juice after you flip them. Remove the tuna from the skillet and slice into ½-inch strips.

3 Remove the noodles from the refrigerator, drizzle over the chimichurri, and then top with the tuna. Drizzle additional chimichurri on top and serve.

For the chimichurri
½ cup packed fresh flat-leaf parsley
½ teaspoon dried oregano
½ cup packed fresh cilantro
2 medium garlic cloves, minced
½ seeded and diced serrano chile or jalapeño
2 tablespoons diced white onion
1½ tablespoons red wine vinegar
2 tablespoons olive oil
   Salt and pepper

2 (4-ounce) ahi tuna fillets
   Salt and cracked black peppercorns
1 tablespoon olive oil
2 tablespoons lime juice
1 large seedless cucumber, spiralized with BLADE D, patted dry and chilled

Pesto Turnips with Shredded Brussels Sprouts

MAKES
3 servings

TIME TO PREPARE
15 minutes

TIME TO COOK
15 minutes

NUTRITIONAL INFORMATION
SERVING SIZE: **2 cups**
Calories: 310
Fat: 26 g
Carbohydrates: 17 g
Sodium: 138 mg
Protein: 4 g
Sugar: 8 g

ALSO WORKS WELL WITH
Parsnips · Zucchini ·
Rutabaga · Butternut
Squash· Beets ·
Celeriac

Turnips can be tricky because they have a distinct radish-like taste. In this recipe, we toss the warm turnip noodles with a robust pesto, thereby enjoying the root vegetable while masking most of its bitterness. The Brussels sprouts offer an almost velvety softness; they also pack a hearty amount of vitamin C, which is an important nutrient during those cold winter months. Keep healthy and curl up with this warm, flavorful pasta.

1 Combine the basil, pine nuts, olive oil, garlic, salt, and pepper in a food processor and pulse until smooth.

2 Halve and then thinly slice the Brussels sprouts to shreds.

3 Heat the olive oil in a large skillet over medium heat. When the oil is shimmering, add the turnip noodles and Brussels sprouts, and season with salt and pepper. Cover and cook for 3 to 5 minutes or until the turnip noodles are al dente, uncovering and tossing occasionally. Transfer to a large bowl. Pour the pesto on top and toss to combine thoroughly. Serve warm.

3 cups packed basil leaves

2 tablespoons pine nuts

¼ cup olive oil

1 large garlic clove, minced

½ teaspoon freshly ground sea salt

¼ teaspoon freshly ground black pepper

2 cups trimmed Brussels sprouts

1 tablespoon extra-virgin olive oil

3 medium turnips, peeled, spiralized with BLADE C

Salt and pepper

Try turning this basil pesto into a cilantro pesto and use pepitas instead of pine nuts.

Tofu Miso-Tahini Carrot Bowl

MAKES
2 servings

TIME TO PREPARE
15 minutes

TIME TO COOK
15 minutes

NUTRITIONAL INFORMATION
SERVING SIZE: **2 cups**
Calories: 494
Fat: 36 g
Carbohydrates: 28 g
Sodium: 1586 mg
Protein: 21 g
Sugar: 10 g

ALSO WORKS WELL WITH
Zucchini · Kohlrabi ·
Broccoli

Tofu is like a sponge; it absorbs flavors very well. One of my favorite ways to prepare tofu is to marinate it in soy sauce and then roast it, as in this recipe. When I was vegan, my go-to dinner was roasted tofu with brown rice and a sautéed vegetable medley. BOR-ing! This meal is much more exciting, but with that same easy tofu. With the thick dressing, the carrot noodles soften slightly and combine with the miso and tahini, while the edamame offers a lean protein and a colorful crunch. This works for lunch or dinner, and also stores well in the refrigerator.

1 Make the dressing. Pulse the ingredients in a food processor until creamy. If necessary, add water a teaspoon at a time until the dressing reaches the desired consistency.

2 Line a plate with two layers of paper towels. Place the tofu cubes on top of the paper towels and add two more layers of paper towels. Gently press down on the tofu, removing excess moisture. Repeat with fresh paper towels.

3 Preheat the oven to 400 degrees. Coat a baking sheet with cooking spray. Place the tofu in a medium bowl with the soy sauce, tossing to coat. Transfer to the baking sheet and roast for 10 to 13 minutes or until lightly browned.

For the dressing
6 tablespoons tahini
2 tablespoons fresh lemon juice
2 tablespoons miso paste
1 tablespoon vegetable oil
1 teaspoon minced garlic
2 teaspoons mirin
   Salt and pepper

½ cup cubed firm tofu
2 tablespoons low-sodium soy sauce
   Cooking spray
2 large carrots, peeled, spiralized with
   BLADE D
⅓ cup frozen edamame beans
1 teaspoon white sesame seeds
¼ cup sunflower sprouts

4 Place a medium saucepan of water over high heat and bring to a boil. Add the carrot noodles and edamame, and cook for 2 minutes or until al dente. Drain well.

5 Place a small skillet over medium-high heat. When a little water flicked onto the skillet sizzles, add the sesame seeds and cook for 2 to 3 minutes, tossing frequently until aromatic and just beginning to brown.

6 In a large bowl, combine the edamame and carrot noodles, and add the sunflower sprouts. Toss with the dressing and top with the tofu and sesame seeds.

If you can't find sunflower sprouts, substitute watercress or pea shoots.

DESSERTS

Pecan and Carrot Almond Butter Bars with Chocolate Drizzle

Pear Rhubarb Crisp

Apple Ambrosia Fruit Salad

No-Bake Plantain Cacao Balls

Plantain Coconut Rice Pudding

Apple and Pear Ricotta Parfaits with Pistachios

Double Chocolate–Pecan Sweet Potato Dessert Pancakes

Blueberry Pear Ice Pops

Chocolate Chip Sweet Potato Muffins

Pecan and Carrot Almond Butter Bars with Chocolate Drizzle

MAKES
8 to 10 bars

GF

V

P

TIME TO PREPARE
30 minutes

NUTRITIONAL INFORMATION
SERVING SIZE: **1 bar**
Calories: 316
Fat: 26 g
Carbohydrates: 19 g
Sodium: 76 mg
Protein: 10 g
Sugar: 11 g

One of the oldest tricks in the book of healthy eating is to always be prepared. By stocking your refrigerator and pantry with nutritious snacks, you're ahead of the game simply because you have no other choice but to eat healthy when you're hungry. These dessert bars have it all: chocolate, crunchy nuts, creamy almond butter, and even some fruit and veggies.

1 Line an 11 x 7-inch baking sheet with parchment paper.

2 In a large bowl, combine the carrot rice, almond butter, maple syrup, pecans, raisins, and a pinch of salt and mix thoroughly.

3 Transfer the carrot rice mixture to the baking sheet and spread in an even layer. Top with plastic wrap and use your hands to press down so that the mixture is uniformly flat, about 1 inch thick. Remove the plastic wrap.

4 Make the drizzle. In a small saucepan over medium heat, melt the chocolate chips and almond milk, whisking continually until the chocolate is melted. If the sauce is too thick, add a bit more milk, 1 tablespoon at a time.

5 Drizzle the chocolate over the carrot rice mixture. Place the baking sheet in the freezer for at least 4 hours. While still frozen, cut into bars. Store refrigerated in an airtight container and serve cold.

2 large carrots, peeled, spiralized with BLADE C, then riced (see page 25)

½ cup whole pecans, roughly chopped

⅓ cup golden raisins

Salt

1 cup creamy almond butter

1 tablespoon pure maple syrup

For the chocolate drizzle

½ cup dairy-free chocolate chips

2 tablespoons almond milk

The bars are easily adaptable to suit your taste; try making them with other nuts, such as almonds and walnuts, or other nut butters, such as hazelnut and peanut.

Pear Rhubarb Crisp

MAKES
4 servings

TIME TO PREPARE
15 minutes

TIME TO COOK
30 minutes

NUTRITIONAL INFORMATION
SERVING SIZE: 1 6-ounce ramekin crisp
Calories: 142
Fat: 2 g
Carbohydrates: 32 g
Sodium: 33 mg
Protein: 3 g
Sugar: 16 g

ALSO WORKS WELL WITH
Apples

Rhubarb is used primarily in baking, yielding an impeccable natural tartness that pairs well with sweet fruit. The combination with pear here is remarkable. And what's the best part of this recipe? You don't have to stand at your kitchen counter, painstakingly slicing the pear with a mandolin or knife—the spiralizer simplifies the process. You'll need four 6-ounce ramekins for this preparation.

1 Preheat the oven to 350 degrees. Coat the inside of four 6-ounce ramekins with cooking spray.

2 Slice the rhubarb, then dice. In a large bowl, toss the rhubarb with the pear noodles, cinnamon, orange juice, and zest.

3 Pack the mixture into the ramekins, filling each three-fourths full. Set the ramekins on a baking sheet and bake for 30 minutes or until the noodles wilt.

4 Top each ramekin with 2 tablespoons of granola and return them to the oven to bake for an additional 5 minutes. Serve immediately.

Cooking spray
3 rhubarb stalks
3 pears, spiralized with BLADE C
1 teaspoon ground cinnamon
3 tablespoons fresh orange juice
Zest of half an orange
½ cup gluten-free granola

Apple Ambrosia Fruit Salad

The summer after I turned vegan, I was living in New York City. One hot day I went on a quest for vegan "ice cream" and found a spot with a sign in the window that read "Dairy Free Organic Yogurt." I came out victorious: a cup of coconut frozen yogurt topped with chunks of apple and pineapple. Although I'm more of a cake person now than an ice cream one, I still dream about those fresh flavors I tasted that day and have re-created them here.

1 Cut the apple vertically halfway to the center, being sure not to pierce the center. Spiralize using blade B.

2 Scoop off the top layer of "cream" from the coconut milk and put into a medium bowl. (Discard the remainder or save for another use.) Add the vanilla, orange juice, and honey and whisk until light and foamy. Add the pineapple, pecans, coconut, and apple noodles and stir thoroughly to combine. Chill in the refrigerator until ready to serve.

1 apple (Gala, or other sweet variety)
1 (14-ounce) can full-fat coconut milk, refrigerated for 24 hours
1 teaspoon vanilla extract
2 tablespoons orange juice
2 teaspoons honey
1 cup diced pineapple
1 cup chopped pecans
½ cup unsweetened coconut flakes

If you're serving this fruit salad at a party, divide it among sundae glasses and garnish with maraschino cherries. Also, note that the apples will absorb more flavor the longer they sit.

No-Bake Plantain Cacao Balls

MAKES
10 to 12 balls

GF

TIME TO PREPARE
20 minutes

V

TIME TO COOK
5 minutes

P

NUTRITIONAL INFORMATION
SERVING SIZE: **1 ball**
Calories: 120
Fat: 1 g
Carbohydrates: 30 g
Sodium: 4 mg
Protein: 1 g
Sugar: 21 g

Having unprocessed sweets and snacks in your house is the key to balanced eating. If you stock your pantry and refrigerator with clean treats, your body and mind will thank you and your mind-set will shift away from "following a diet" and toward living a lifestyle. These easy, no-bake balls are exactly that—made with real, whole ingredients, and only five of them. They won't give you a sugar crash, and the plantain's starchiness helps bind everything and keep you fueled longer. Snack on these no-bake balls to satisfy your sweet tooth and give you that energy boost.

1 Place a large nonstick skillet over medium-high heat. When a little water flicked onto the skillet sizzles, add the plantain rice and cook for 3 minutes, tossing frequently, until browned. Remove the pan from the heat and set aside.

2 Pulse the dates in a food processor until paste-like, about 1 minute. If the dates don't break down easily, add a little water, 1 teaspoon at a time. Add the plantain rice, the cacao, and coconut flakes and continue to pulse until the mixture is sticky and smooth.

3 Transfer the mixture to a medium bowl and add the pepitas, mixing by hand until blended well. Form 10 to 12 balls that are 1 inch in diameter and refrigerate for at least 15 minutes before serving.

2 plantains, peeled, spiralized with BLADE C, and riced (see page 25)

10 Medjool dates, pitted and roughly chopped

2 teaspoons raw cacao powder

1½ tablespoons unsweetened coconut flakes

3 teaspoons roasted and salted pepitas (Mexican pumpkin seeds)

Plantain Coconut Rice Pudding

MAKES
1 serving

GF

V

P

TIME TO PREPARE
15 minutes

TIME TO COOK
10 minutes

NUTRITIONAL INFORMATION
SERVING SIZE: 1$\frac{1}{2}$–
2 heaping cups
Calories: 476
Carbohydrates: 112 g
Sodium: 212 mg
Protein: 5 g
Sugar: 71 g

I never liked rice pudding until I met this recipe. Here, the coconut meshes organically with the slight sweetness of the plantain and the creaminess of the almond milk, hence a warm balance results. The raisins and cinnamon invoke that classic rice pudding aroma and flavor, too. Everything comes together in this lightened version of the classic, now a simple vegan dessert that's ideal for an after-dinner treat.

1 In a medium saucepan over high heat, combine the plantain rice and 1 cup of the almond milk. Bring to a boil, then lower the heat and simmer for 10 minutes or until the liquid reduces to the point that the rice begins to stick to the bottom of the pan. Add the remaining $\frac{1}{3}$ cup almond milk and simmer to reduce again, stirring occasionally until the mixture is creamy, about 3 minutes.

2 Remove the pan from the heat and add the cinnamon, coconut flakes, and raisins. Stir until the cinnamon dissolves into the pudding. Serve hot.

1 medium-ripe plantain, peeled, spiralized with BLADE C, then riced (see page 25)

1$\frac{1}{3}$ cups vanilla almond milk

$\frac{1}{8}$ teaspoon ground cinnamon

1 to 2 teaspoons unsweetened coconut flakes

$\frac{1}{4}$ cup raisins

If you don't have access to vanilla almond milk or prefer to use a milk type that's not flavored, just add 1 teaspoon vanilla extract to the mix.

Apple and Pear Ricotta Parfaits with Pistachios

MAKES
2 servings

TIME TO PREPARE
10 minutes

NUTRITIONAL INFORMATION
SERVING SIZE: 1½ cups
Calories: 485
Fat: 19 g
Carbohydrates: 75 g
Sodium: 203 mg
Protein: 14 g
Sugar: 58 g

Every time I see a parfait at a coffee shop or a grocery store, I cringe. They look so lifeless! There's never been anything special about them—until now. These fruit noodles are fresh and crunchy; the ricotta whipped with honey and vanilla adds a creamy, sweet consistency.

1 In a medium bowl, whisk together the ricotta, honey, and vanilla until light and fluffy.

2 Evenly divide the raspberry jam into two parfait glasses. Layer on the ricotta, and add the apple and pear noodles. Sprinkle the pistachios on top and serve immediately.

½ cup ricotta cheese

2 tablespoons honey

1 teaspoon vanilla extract

¼ cup raspberry jam

1 apple, spiralized with BLADE C

1 pear, spiralized with BLADE C

½ cup roughly chopped roasted and salted pistachios

Convert this dessert parfait into a breakfast parfait by swapping plain nonfat Greek yogurt for the ricotta.

Double Chocolate–Pecan Sweet Potato Dessert Pancakes

MAKES
2 pancakes

GF

VT

TIME TO PREPARE
20 minutes

TIME TO COOK
15 minutes

NUTRITIONAL INFORMATION
SERVING SIZE:
1 pancake
Calories: 381
Fat: 24 g
Carbohydrates: 34 g
Sodium: 80 mg
Protein: 9 g
Sugar: 18 g

More often than not, when I go out for brunch I face a mental struggle: *Do I get the cinnamon swirl french toast with chocolate drizzle or the egg white scramble*? Nine times out of ten I make the healthy choice—but that one other time I enjoy every last bite of the indulgence. With these pancakes made from sweet potatoes, though, I don't have to struggle! Not only are they clean-eating friendly, but they're also satisfying—the natural sugar in the sweet potatoes is released and creates a pancake that's seemingly decadent *and* miraculously nutritious. Everyone loves breakfast for dinner, so why not make breakfast for dessert?

Cooking spray

1 large sweet potato, peeled, spiralized with BLADE C

2 fresh strawberries, hulled and chopped

¼ cup roughly chopped pecans

2 teaspoons honey

3 tablespoons plain nonfat Greek yogurt

1 tablespoon raw cacao powder

1 medium egg, lightly beaten

1 teaspoon vanilla extract

2 tablespoons dairy-free dark chocolate chips

1 tablespoon olive oil

1 Place a large nonstick skillet over medium heat and coat with cooking spray. When a little water flicked onto the skillet sizzles, add the sweet potato noodles and cover. Cook, turning occasionally, for 5 to 7 minutes or until the sweet potato noodles have softened and are lightly browned.

2 Combine the strawberries, pecans, honey, and yogurt in a medium bowl. Set in the refrigerator to briefly chill.

3 Transfer the sweet potato noodles to a large bowl and add the cacao, egg, vanilla, and chocolate chips. Toss to blend well.

4 Return the skillet to medium heat and add half the olive oil. When the oil is shimmering, add half the sweet potato mixture to the center of the skillet. Using a spatula, quickly flatten into a pancake. Cook for about 2 minutes or until the bottom is set, then flip the pancake over, flatten again with a spatula, and cook for 2 minutes more or until completely set. Transfer to a plate. Repeat with remaining ½ tablespoon olive oil and remaining pancake mix.

5 Top the pancakes with the strawberry-yogurt mixture and serve.

If you prefer, you can easily turn these pancakes into dessert waffles simply by packing the noodle mixture into a waffle iron.

Blueberry Pear Ice Pops

MAKES
10 ice pops

GF

TIME TO PREPARE
8 hours+

VT

NUTRITIONAL INFORMATION
SERVING SIZE: **1 ice pop**
Calories: 41
Fat: 0
Carbohydrates: 10 g
Sodium: 4 mg
Protein: 1 g
Sugar: 7 g

I have always preferred yogurts with real chunks of fruit at the bottom. After all, clean eating is all about consuming foods as close to whole as possible. So ditch the commercial ice pops that are made with juice concentrate, and make these amazing yogurt ones that present a real fruit surprise. When the popsicle starts to melt, the pear noodles "pop" through!

1 Place the yogurt, blueberries, and honey in a food processor and pulse until creamy. Trim the pear noodles so that they are no more than 3 or 4 inches long.

2 For each ice pop mold, put in a thin layer of pear noodles and then cover with some blueberry filling. Add another thin layer of pear noodles, pushing the noodles down into the yogurt mixture.

3 Insert the ice pop sticks and freeze for at least 8 hours. To release the ice pops from the mold, very briefly run the mold under hot water.

1 cup vanilla nonfat Greek yogurt
1 cup fresh blueberries
1 tablespoon honey
2 ripe pears, peeled, spiralized with
   BLADE D

If you don't have ice pop molds and sticks on hand, you can still make this dessert. Fill a shot glass or small cup with the filling, insert a sturdy straw in the center, and freeze.

Chocolate Chip Sweet Potato Muffins

MAKES
6 muffins

GF

VT

P

TIME TO PREPARE
10 minutes

TIME TO COOK
25 minutes

NUTRITIONAL INFORMATION
SERVING SIZE: **1 muffin**
Calories: 132
Fat: 6 g
Carbohydrates: 18 g
Sodium: 137 mg
Protein: 3 g
Sugar: 12 g

I made these muffins for a road trip I was taking with friends from high school. When everyone had piled in and settled into the backseat of my car, I whipped these out. The muffins got thumbs-up all around! Flourless, moist, and chocolately, they came to be my trusty after-dinner treat and they won't cause a sugar crash later.

1 Preheat the oven to 375 degrees. Coat a 6-cup muffin tin lightly with cooking spray.

2 Combine the sweet potato rice, cinnamon, baking soda, coconut flakes, and a pinch of salt in a medium bowl. Add the egg and egg white, honey, and vanilla and mix thoroughly. Fold in the chocolate chips.

3 Spoon the batter into the cups, filling each three-fourths of the way. Bake for 23 to 25 minutes or until a knife inserted in the center of a muffin comes out clean. Remove the muffins from the tin and allow to cool on a rack for 5 minutes before serving.

Cooking spray

1 small sweet potato, peeled, spiralized with BLADE C, then riced (1 cup; see page 25)

½ teaspoon ground cinnamon

½ teaspoon baking soda

2 tablespoons unsweetened coconut flakes

Salt

1 large egg plus 1 egg white

2 tablespoons honey

½ teaspoon vanilla extract

5 tablespoons dairy-free chocolate chips (such as Enjoy Life)

The muffins are more moist than regular muffins because they are flourless. To prevent wet bottoms, allow them to rest for at least 30 minutes before storing in an airtight container.

FRUITS
AND
VEGGIES
A to Z

Apple

The best part about spiralizing this fruit is that each different type of apple yields a unique flavor. Some apples, like Gala, are sweeter and some, like Granny Smith, are more sour. Apples spiralize very easily—the only preparation required is removing the stem. If you find that the apple stops spiralizing halfway through, simply flip it around, secure from the other end, and continue.

IMPORTANT NUTRIENTS: vitamin C

Beet

Don't be afraid to stain your spiralizer with beets—just rinse and scrub it with soap and water immediately after use. When beets are turned into noodles, they roast much faster than when they're whole, which makes them ideal for quick cooking. You can also spiralize roasted whole beets. Treat golden and red beets the same way—and their green tips can be incorporated alongside the noodles.

IMPORTANT NUTRIENTS: folate and manganese

Broccoli

Most are surprised by the fact that, yes, you can spiralize a broccoli stem. When buying a head of broccoli for spiralizing, make sure that the stem is as thick and long as possible, at least 1.5 inches wide and 5 to 6 inches long for maximum results. When you remove the florets from the stem when preparing to spiralize, it's important to not waste much of the stem. You can save the broccoli florets for another use, but using them in the recipe enhances the flavor of their stem's noodles.

IMPORTANT NUTRIENTS: vitamin C, potassium, and calcium

Butternut squash

When choosing butternut squashes for spiralizing, try your best to find those with a small bulbous bottom. Remember, you must always slice that part off, since it has a seedy core and cannot be spiralized. It won't go to waste, though—dice it into cubes and save it for another use. If your butternut squash is very large, halve it before loading it onto the spiralizer for best results. If the noodles stick together, carefully pull them apart afterward.

IMPORTANT NUTRIENTS: vitamins A and C

Carrot

The toughest part of spiralizing carrots is finding those that are large enough. An ideal carrot diameter is 2 inches. This vegetable's naturally sweet taste makes it perfect for light sauces as well as dishes with salty foods like feta cheese and olives. When boiled, carrots have a similar consistency to whole-wheat pasta.

IMPORTANT NUTRIENTS: vitamin A and beta-carotene

Cabbage

Spiralizing a cabbage won't yield cabbage noodles, but it is an easier, quicker way to "shred" the vegetable. There's no preparation required and by simply running it through the spiralizer, you'll have shredded cabbage, best for using in slaws and salads.

IMPORTANT NUTRIENTS: vitamins C and K

Celeriac

Celeriac—the root that celery grows on—has the same tart, herbal taste as the commonly eaten stalks. Celeriac really looks like it grows in the ground—it's lumpy, tough, and difficult to peel. Once peeled, it takes maximum effort in the spiralizer, but the noodles have an earthy freshness that's wonderful with thick sauces and heavy proteins.

IMPORTANT NUTRIENTS: vitamins C and K and phosphorus

Chayote

Chayotes are native to Mexico but are cultivated in similarly warm climates worldwide. Popular in Central American cuisine, as well as in the southern United States, they are also referred to as pear squash, mirletons, cho-cho, chouchoute, or choko. The noodles look almost identical to those of the zucchini. Although technically a fruit, chayotes have a similarly mild taste to that of zucchini, but don't yield quite as much moisture. Chayotes require no preparation and make ideal spirals.

IMPORTANT NUTRIENTS: vitamin C, folate, and zinc

Cucumber

Cucumbers, normally just diced or cubed and tossed in salads, take on a new life with the spiralizer. They release a lot of excess moisture, however, so they must be patted very dry after spiralizing and before they're incorporated into a recipe.

IMPORTANT NUTRIENTS: hydration and vitamin K

Jícama

Native to Mexico and Central and South Americas, jícama is a nutrient-dense root vegetable low in calories. With similar crispness and moistness to an apple, jícama has a lightly sweet and nutty flavor. It is typically used as a raw garnish or in salad, but spiralizing gives us the opportunity to turn them into much more.

IMPORTANT NUTRIENTS: vitamin C

Kohlrabi

Kohlrabis come in two different variations—white and purple—but both have a similar creamy yellow-colored flesh. While peeling a kohlrabi can be a little tricky, it spiralizes effortlessly. The greens can be cooked right alongside its spiralized noodles. Kohlrabis taste like a fresh, crunchy broccoli stem with a hint of cucumber and are very versatile.

IMPORTANT NUTRIENTS: fiber and vitamin C

Onion

The spiralizer can be used to shred onions, which is best for hashes or to make noodles for caramelizing, baking into onion rings, and for tossing into salads. Typically, sliced onions have a lighter, more subtle taste when spiralized into noodles. Any type of large onion can be used: yellow, white, sweet Vidalia, or red.

IMPORTANT NUTRIENTS: biotin (a vitamin B type) and manganese

Parsnip

Parsnips have a wonderfully nutty and sweet flavor when cooked, ideal for gratins and casseroles. They taper in shape, so look for one with a thick top, or one that is as uniform in shape as possible. Prior to loading the parsnip onto the spiralizer, slice off any part of the parsnip that is less than 1 inch in diameter and save for another use.

IMPORTANT NUTRIENTS: vitamin C, fiber, and manganese

Pear

Like apples, pears spiralize easily and require only the removal of the stem as preparation. They have velvety smooth flesh that's wonderful when paired with whole grains or tough proteins, like steaks. Each type of pear has a different flavor; Bosc pears are softer than Concorde, for example, and have honey and vanilla hints, respectively.

IMPORTANT NUTRIENTS: fiber and vitamin C

Plantain

Plantains are the staple sources of carbohydrates for large populations in Asia, Africa, the Caribbean, and Central and South Americas. The toughest food to spiralize, plantains are a bit of a stretch. However, they are extremely flavorful and therefore ideal in desserts. Plantains can be peeled using a knife or a peeler, but be careful not to slice off too much flesh.

IMPORTANT NUTRIENTS: vitamins A and C and potassium

Potato

Russet, white, and yellow potatoes all work well in the spiralizer. With russet potatoes, some moisture will seep out and can stain the spiralizer, so be sure to clean the tool immediately after use.

IMPORTANT NUTRIENTS: vitamin C and potassium

Radish

Radishes, with their typically soapy and bitter taste and smell, are transformed when spiralized. They are best used in soups, since they offer a fantastic crunch and absorb the flavors in the broth, masking their bite. Daikons (Asian radishes) are typically thick and long, ideal for spiralizing. Small red radishes will work well too!

IMPORTANT NUTRIENTS: vitamin C, potassium, and folate

Rutabaga

Also known as swedes or wax turnips, rutabagas spiralize into long, sturdy spirals. They tend to be large, so just one rutabaga yields several servings of noodles. In the same family as turnips and cabbage, they are mild and become sweeter when cooked. Rutabagas are resilient and can withstand all types of sauces and cooking methods.

IMPORTANT NUTRIENTS: vitamin C and potassium

Sweet potato or yam

Sweet potatoes and yams have a distinct, sweet taste that comes through when used in pasta and noodle dishes. They absorb liquids, so they work well with heavy pasta sauces, like a pomodoro. Since their flesh is tough, it takes some elbow grease to spiralize them, but they're well worth it. Never boil sweet potato noodles, because they will break apart into pieces.

IMPORTANT NUTRIENTS: vitamins B_6 and C and iron

Turnip

Turnips are a root vegetable with a slightly bitter flavor that can easily be masked by distinct sauces and dressings, such as a pesto. When buying turnips for spiralizing, be sure to find large, round ones to yield better spirals. Sautéed turnip noodles have an al dente pasta-like consistency. Due to their high water content, turnips might need to be drained prior to being cooked as rice. Just use your hands to squeeze out the liquid.

IMPORTANT NUTRIENTS: vitamin C and calcium

Yuca or Cassava Root

The tremendously tough flesh of yuca makes it difficult to spiralize. Not only is it tricky to get enough leverage, but the noodles also come out slightly shredded and uneven. Once spiralized, yuca can be sautéed but will soften and may not hold well. It works in desserts with natural sugars and other sweet add-ons. If you're a yuca lover and want to spiralize it, please do, but because it's not an ideal candidate for spiralizing, I haven't included any yuca recipes in this cookbook.

IMPORTANT NUTRIENTS: potassium

Zucchini and Summer Squash

Zucchini and yellow squash are the most popularly spiralized vegetables for a reason. Their soft but firm flesh is ideal for that al dente pasta texture. Both vegetables have a mild taste, perfect for pairing with light sauces and for being used in pasta salads. Their only downfall is their high water content, so when they hit a warm sauce, they release liquid that can cause an unpleasant watery consistency. To best avoid this, see page 27 for tips. If you can't find large zucchinis out of season, use blade A to yield the most noodles possible.

IMPORTANT NUTRIENTS: manganese, vitamin C, and folates

Nutritional Information of Vegetable Noodles

All of this nutritional data was calculated using the USDA National Nutrient Database for Standard Reference.

	Calories (G)	Carbs (G)	Fat (G)	Protein (G)	Sugar (G)
Beet (medium)	64.5	15	0.3	2.4	10.5
Broccoli stem (large)	68	14	0.8	5.6	3.4
Butternut squash (large)	81	21.6	0.18	1.8	3.96
Carrot (large)	77.9	19	0.38	1.71	8.93
Celeriac (large)	86.52	18.54	0.618	3.09	3.296
Chayote	38	9	0.2	1.6	3.2
Cucumber (large)	30.4	6.84	0.19	1.14	3.23
Daikon radish (large)	34.2	7.6	0	1.9	5.7
Jícama (medium)	89.3	21.15	0.235	1.645	4.23
Kohlrabi (medium)	71.82	15.96	0.266	4.522	6.916
Parsnip (large)	120	28.8	0.48	1.92	7.68
Plantain (large)	122	32	0.4	1.3	15
Rutabaga (large)	62.7	14.85	0.33	1.815	7.425
Sweet potato (large)	141.9	33	0	2.64	6.93
Turnip (large)	60.2	12.9	0.215	1.935	8.17
White potato (large)	134.3	30.6	0.17	3.57	1.02
Zucchini (medium)	41.65	7.595	0.735	2.94	6.125

Noodle Yields and Sizes

Each noodle serving comes to about 1½ to 2 cups cooked, depending on the vegetable or fruit.

	Vegetable/Fruit Size (G)	Noodle Yield (G)	Noodle Serving (G)
Apple (medium)	195	150	N/A
Beet (medium)	248	150	150
Broccoli stem (Large)	352	200	200
Butternut squash (large)	2074	870	180
Carrot (large)	500	363	190
Celeriac (large)	573	475	206
Chayote	200	200	200
Cucumber (large)	398	300	190
Daikon radish (large)	601	500	190
Jícama (medium)	752	546	235

	Vegetable/Fruit Size (G)	Noodle Yield (G)	Noodle Serving (G)
Kohlrabi (medium)	385	266	266
Onion (medium)	230	164	N/A
Parsnip (large)	251	160	160
Pear (medium)	304	215	N/A
Plantain (large)	340	155	155g
Rutabaga (large)	905	767	165
Sweet potato large)	407	335	135
Turnip (large)	320	215	215
White potatoes (large)	536	700	170
Zucchini (medium)	298	280	245

Best Practices for Spiralizing Fruit and Veggies

Veggie/Fruit	Prep	Raw or Cooked	Cook Method	Cook Time (min)	Best Served As	Best Blade
Apple	Remove stem.	Both	Bake at 400°	10	Snack, dessert	A
			Sauté in skillet	6–7	Snack, dessert	A
			Raw	N/A	Salad add-on	C
Beet	Peel and slice off ends.	Both	Sauté in skillet	6–8	Pasta, noodles	C, D
			Boil	3–4	Pasta, noodles, soup	C, B
			Bake at 375°	25–30	Chips	A
			Simmer	6–8	Rice	C, B
			Bake at 425°	5–10	Pasta, noodles	C
			Raw	N/A	Noodles, salad add-on, snack	C, D
Broccoli stem	Peel to make an even skin surface.	Cooked	Sauté in skillet	6–7	Pasta, noodles, snack	C, D
			Boil	2–3	Pasta, noodles, snack, soup	C, D
Butternut squash	Peel, slice off ends, and chop in half.	Cooked	Bake at 400°	8–10	Pasta, noodles	C, D
			Sauté in skillet	10	Pasta, noodles, rice	C
			Bake at 375°	25–30	Chips	A
Cabbage	Remove outer layers and slice in half.	Raw or Cooked	Sauté in skillet	4–5	Hot salad, hash	A
			Raw	N/A	Salad add-on, slaw, soup	A

(continued)

Veggie/Fruit	Prep	Raw or Cooked	Cook Method	Cook Time (min)	Best Served As	Best Blade
Carrot	Peel, slice off ends, and chop in half.	Both	Boil	3–4	Pasta, noodles, soup	C, B, D
			Simmer	5–7	Pasta, noodles	C, B, D
			Bake at 425°	10–15	Fries, chips	A, B, C
			Simmer	7–10	Rice	C, D
			Bake at 400°	10	Pasta, noodles	C, D
			Raw	N/A	Salad add-on, slaw	C, D
Celeriac	Chop off ends of the root, peel, and chop in half if large.	Cooked	Sauté in skillet	6–7	Pasta, noodles, bun	C, D
			Bake at 400°	10–15	Pasta, noodles	C
			Simmer	6–7	Rice, soup	C
			Bake at 425°	15	Fries, chips	All
Chayote	Slice off ends and chop in half.	Both	Sauté in skillet	2–3	Pasta, noodles	All
			Simmer	2	Noodles, soup	All
			Raw	N/A	Pasta, noodles, salad add-on, slaw	All
Cucumber	Slice off ends and chop in half and press in between paper towels to remove excess moisture.	Raw	Press in between paper towels to remove excess moisture	Can be served immediately	Noodles, salad add-ons, soup	All
Daikon radish	Peel, slice off ends, and chop in half.	Both	Sauté in skillet	6-7	Pasta, noodles, bun	C
			Simmer	5	Soup	B, C, D
			Simmer	6–7	Rice	C
			Raw	N/A	Salad add-on, noodles	C
Jícama	Peel, slice off ends, and chop in half.	Both	Sauté in skillet	6–7	Pasta, noodles, bun	C
			Bake at 400°	10–12	Pasta, noodles	C
			Simmer	6–7	Rice	C
			Bake at 425°	15–20	Fries, chips	A, B
			Raw	N/A	Salad add-on, slaw, soup	C
Kohlrabi	Peel, slice off ends, and chop in half if large.	Both	Sauté in skillet	6–8	Pasta, noodles, bun	C, D
			Bake at 425°	10–15	Fries, chips	A, B
			Simmer	3–4	Soup	B, C, D
Onion	Peel the outer papery layers of skin and chop off the ends.	Both	Sauté in skillet	3–4	Addition to a stir-fry, salad, soup	A
			Bake at 415°	15–20	Onion rings or fries	C
			Raw	N/A	Salad add-on, slaw, soup	A, D

Veggie/Fruit	Prep	Raw or Cooked	Cook Method	Cook Time (min)	Best Served As	Best Blade
Parsnip	Peel, slice off ends, and chop in half.	Cooked	Saute in skillet	6–7	Pasta, Noodles, Bun	C, D
			Bake at 400°	10–12	Pasta, Noodles	C
			Simmer	6–7	Rice	C
			Bake at 425°	15–20	Fries, Chips	A, B
Pear	Chop off the ends.	Both	Sauté in skillet	6–7	Snack, dessert	A
			Bake at 400°	8–10	Snack, dessert	A
			Raw	N/A	Salad add-on	C
Plantain	Slice off the ends, peel, and chop in half.	Cooked	Simmer	6–7	Rice	C
			Bake at 415°	15	Fries, chips	All
Potato	Peel, slice off ends, and chop in half if large.	Cooked	Sauté in skillet	6–8	Pasta, noodles	C, D
			Simmer	5–7	Pasta, noodles	C, D
			Bake at 425°	15–20	Fries, chips	All
Rutabaga	Peel, slice off ends, and chop in half.	Cooked	Sauté in skillet	6–8	Pasta, noodles, bun	C, D
			Simmer	5–7	Pasta, noodles, soup	C, D
			Simmer	7–10	Rice	C
			Bake at 425°	15–20	Pasta, noodles	C, B
Sweet potato	Peel, slice off ends, and chop in half if large.	Cooked	Sauté in skillet	6–8	Pasta, noodles, bun	C, D
			Simmer	5–7	Pasta, noodles	C, D
			Bake at 425°	10–15	Pasta, noodles	C, B
Turnip	Chop off ends of the root and peel.	Cooked	Sauté in skillet	6–7	Pasta, noodles, soup	C, D
			Bake at 400°	10–12	Pasta, noodles	C
			Simmer	6–7	Rice	C, D
Zucchini, yellow squash	Slice off ends and chop in half	Both	Sauté in skillet	2–3	Pasta, noodles	All
			Simmer	2	Noodles, soup	All
			Raw	N/A	Pasta, noodles, salad add-on, slaw	All

ACKNOWLEDGMENTS

For my first twenty-six years, I was living a life that followed the "appropriate" track: do well in school, go to a notable college, get a job after graduation, and build a career. A few months after my twenty-sixth birthday, I quit my job and took a leap of faith in pursuit of a dream to make the world a happier and healthier place with Inspiralized.com. Now, just less than two years later, I am publishing my first cookbook, at age twenty-seven. Pinch me, please!

Without the support and love around me, I would never have achieved such success, especially in such little time. I would still be dreaming—not doing—and for that, I am eternally grateful to the following people:

Leah Bhabha, thank you for testing every single recipe in this book, responding to my texts at all hours, and being a fellow lover of all foods. Since we spent the larger part of our summer indoors in my kitchen, I think we owe ourselves a trip to the beach!

To every single reader, follower, and lover of Inspiralized—thank you, thank you, thank you. Every single "like" you've given me on Facebook, every blog post of mine you've retweeted, and every friend you've tagged on my Instagram has brought me here. I'm honored that you've trusted me enough to bring my recipes into your home and among your friends and family. Thank you for being truly Inspiralized.

Amanda Englander, thank you for guiding me through the publishing process as my editor. Thanks for entertaining all of my questions (no matter how obvious the answers were) and expediting the publication of this book—I can't wait to see it sitting on a bookshelf, finally in stores. Of course, thanks to the entire Clarkson Potter team, who I consider to be pioneers, believing in me and Inspiralized at such an early stage. Thanks for bringing my message to the masses!

Alyssa Reuben, thanks for supporting me every step of the way and believing in this spiralizing movement before anyone truly cared. This book is a result of your faith in me, and I'm forever appreciative to have you as my agent. Here's to many more books! Special thanks to Evan and Marisa Richheimmer for connecting Alyssa and me—you two were my original supporters!

To the entire photography crew that made this cookbook gorgeous—I'm still stunned. Thank you to Evan Sung for your incredible ability to capture spiralized vegetables and fruits, and for your kind, composed attitude throughout the experience. Thanks to Chelsea Zimmer for styling the vegetable noodles better than I can and Kaitlyn DuRoss for styling not only the photos but also me (I'm still finding pins in my shirts!).

Felicia, thank you for helping me spread the word about Inspiralized from the very beginning. I'm proud of the caring and loving person you've become, and I can't thank you enough for being there when I needed to vent, helping me plan a wedding while this book came to fruition, and for being my lifelong best friend. You'll always be my "little sister."

Dad, thanks for teaching me there are no shortcuts in life: just hard work, commitment, and determination. Without that, I would still be sitting at a desk, working a job that didn't fulfill me. You are the hardest-working man I have ever known, and I am grateful for every lesson in life you ever taught me. I'm proud to join the family ranks as an entrepreneur!

Grandma Ida, I thank you each and every day for teaching me to love reading and writing. Thank you for spending the countless hours with me, studying the literary classics and helping me to understand the way words come together when I struggled. Your faith in education and knowledge has led me to this hopefully never-ending chapter of my life.

Mom, I could write for hundreds of pages about how thankful I am to have you in my life and never do you justice. There is no one in this world who encourages, supports, and believes in me as much as you do. Not only am I forever grateful to you for introducing me to spiralizing, but I'm thankful for the hours and hours we've talked about living a healthy lifestyle—despite falling off the wagon a few times! You're my best friend, and knowing that I can come to you and talk about anything is more valuable to me than anything else. You've helped me write this book even when you weren't there. Nothing makes me happier than making you proud—this cookbook is as much yours as it is mine. I love you.

Pops, not only do I thank you for every last flawless meatball you put on my plate, but I thank you for being as strong as you are. From walking countless miles in the snow to court Grandma in your twenties to winning a very scary battle with cancer, your love and passion for life has always inspired me to live one that exceeds expectations and puts a smile on my face—and hopefully, on yours. You're my first true love and you'll always be my Poppy.

Grandma Loretta (Grams), you're the life of the party, the brightest smile in the room (and the best dressed!), and the most compassionate woman. Your faith and confidence in those you love is inspirational, and although you always manage to burn the sweet potatoes at Thanksgiving, you are the adorable glue that holds everyone together.

And Lu. When this book hits shelves, we'll be four months away from becoming husband and wife. You're the love of my life, and without you, the whole idea for Inspiralized would never have become what it is today. You encouraged me to quit my job and pursue this dream, believing that I could do anything. Your unwavering faith in me brings tears to my eyes and I can't wait to spend the rest of my life with you, making you as happy as you've made me. You not only lift me up but you also keep me there if I ever start to fall. Every single day, I'm inspired and motivated by your own hard work as an entrepreneur, and I couldn't ask for a better person to have along for the ride in this dream journey. Most important, thank you for genuinely loving healthy food—you might even love zucchini noodles more than I do (doubtful, but maybe!).

A

Almond Butter
    Bars, Pecan and Carrot, with
        Chocolate Drizzle, *192*, 194
    Sesame, Kohlrabi Bowl, 167
Apple(s), 209
    Ambrosia Fruit Salad, 196, *197*
    and Kohlrabi Slaw with Lemon-Mint
        Chia Seed Dressing, 71
    and Pear Ricotta Parfaits with
        Pistachios, *200*, 201
    -Potato Cheese Bun, 119
    with Shaved Asparagus,
        Gorgonzola, and Pecans, 92, *93*
Arugula
    Feta, and Red Wine Vinaigrette,
        Cucumber Noodle Salad with,
        97
    Olive, and Onion Sweet Potato
        Pizza Stacks, *116*, 117–18
Asparagus, Shaved, Gorgonzola, and
    Pecans, Apples with, 92, *93*
Avocado(s)
    Beet Rice Nori Rolls with Chipotle-
        Teriyaki Sauce, 106, *107*
    Beet Superfood Bowl, 140, *141*
    and Chorizo Zucchini Frittata with
        Manchego–Pea Shoot Salad,
        36, 36–37
    Collard Hummus Wraps with
        Golden Beets and Sprouts, 111
    Cucumber, and Strawberry Salsa,
        58, *59*
    Huevos Rancheros, *44*, 45–46
    -Lime Mason Jar Salad, 86–87, *87*
    -Mango Cucumber Spring Rolls
        with Sriracha-Lime Dipping
        Sauce, 73
    Savoy Cabbage Breakfast Burrito,
        50, 51
    Spicy Butternut Squash Nachos,
        60–61

B

Bacon
    Cacio e Pepe, 168, *169*
    Lemon Garlic Broccoli with, *64*,
        65
    Savoy Cabbage Breakfast Burrito,
        50, 51

Sweet Potato Carbonara, 185
Bars, Pecan and Carrot Almond
    Butter, with Chocolate Drizzle,
    192, 194
Basil
    Caprese Zucchini Salad, *84*, 85
    Pesto Spaghetti with Heirloom
        Grape Tomatoes, 170
    Pesto Sun-dried Tomato Egg
        Muffins, 38–39
    Pesto Turnips with Shredded
        Brussels Sprouts, *188*, 189
Beans
    Beet Superfood Bowl, 140, *141*
    Huevos Rancheros, *44*, 45–46
    Spicy Butternut Squash Nachos,
        60–61
    Tilapia Tostadas with Tomato-Corn
        Salsa, 102–3
    Vegetarian Carrot Enchilada Bake,
        127–28, *129*
    Vegetarian Chana Masala with
        Kohlrabi, 159–60, *161*
Beef
    Albondigas and Chayote with
        Tomato-Serrano Sauce, *178*,
        179–80
    Celeriac Chili, Cajun, 79
    Daikon Ramen with Skirt Steak,
        80–81, *81*
    Short Ribs with Sweet Potato
        "Grits," 142
    Steak and Pear Kale Salad, 83
Beet(s), 209
    and Feta Skillet Bake,
        Mediterranean, 122, *123*
    Goat Cheese, and Pomegranate
        Endive Cups, 72, *72*
    Golden, and Sprouts, Collard
        Hummus Wraps with, 111
    Pasta with Blood Orange, Honey
        Walnuts, and Crispy Kale,
        164–66, *165*
    Rice Nori Rolls with Chipotle-
        Teriyaki Sauce, 106, *107*
    for spiralized rice, 24
    Superfood Bowl, 140, *141*
Bhaji, Baked Onion, with Mint-
    Cucumber Raita, 66–67

Blueberry
    Pear Ice Pops, 204, *205*
    Sweet Potato Waffles, 40, *41*
Broccoli, 209
    and Chicken Skillet Bake, 137
    -Gruyère Bread Crumbs, Rutabaga
        Turkey Casserole with, 130
    Lemon Garlic, with Bacon, *64*, 65
    Teriyaki Salmon Balls with Ginger-
        Pineapple Rice, 147–48, *149*
Broccolini, Vegan Celeriac Alfredo
    with, 182–84, *183*
Brussels Sprouts, Shredded, Pesto
    Turnips with, *188*, 189
Buns
    Apple-Potato Cheese, 119
    "Everything Bagel" Breakfast,
        47–48, *49*
    spiralized, how to make, 26
Burgers, Jalapeño Turkey, with
    Cilantro-Lime Kohlrabi, 114–15
Burrito, Savoy Cabbage Breakfast,
    50, 51

C

Cabbage, 209
Cabbage, Savoy, Breakfast Burrito,
    50, 51
Carrot(s), 209
    Bowl, Tofu Miso–Tahini, 190–91
    Chicken Banh Mi with Sriracha
        Greek Yogurt, *108*, 109–10
    Enchilada Bake, Vegetarian, 127–28,
        129
    Mac and Cheese, Vegan Chipotle,
        131
    Noodle Chicken Soup, 76, *77*
    and Pecan Almond Butter Bars
        with Chocolate Drizzle, *192*, 194
    Spicy Seafood-Chorizo Paella, 154,
        155
    for spiralized rice, 24
    Teriyaki Salmon Balls with Ginger-
        Pineapple Rice, 147–48, *149*
Cashews
    Vegan Chipotle Carrot Mac and
        Cheese, 131
Cauliflower Tabouleh Salad, *94*,
    95–96

Celeriac, 210
    Alfredo, Vegan, with Broccolini,
        182–84, *183*
    Beef Chili, Cajun, 79
    for spiralized rice, 24
    Stuffed Grape Leaves Casserole,
        134–35, *135*
Chayote, 210
Chayote and Albondigas with
    Tomato-Serrano Sauce, *178,*
    179–80
Cheese
    Apple and Pear Ricotta Parfaits with
        Pistachios, *200,* 201
    Apples with Shaved Asparagus,
        Gorgonzola, and Pecans, 92, *93*
    Arugula, Olive, and Onion Sweet
        Potato Pizza Stacks, *116,* 117–18
    Bacon Cacio e Pepe, 168, *169*
    Balsamic Glazed Peaches with
        Prosciutto and Roquefort, *68,*
        69–70
    Bun, Apple-Potato, 119
    Caprese Zucchini Salad, *84,* 85
    Chicken and Broccoli Skillet Bake,
        137
    Cucumber Noodle Salad with
        Feta, Arugula, and Red Wine
        Vinaigrette, 97
    Deconstructed Zucchini Manicotti,
        124, 125–26
    Goat, Beet, and Pomegranate
        Endive Cups, 72, *72*
    Goat, Farro, Cherries, and Walnuts,
        Pears with, *62,* 63
    Jícama-Stuffed Peppers with
        Asiago, *156,* 157–58
    Mediterranean Beet and Feta
        Skillet Bake, 122, *123*
    Parsnip and Kale Gratin, *132,* 133
    Pear, Fontina, and Fig Salad with
        Honey-Pistachio Balsamic, 89
    Rutabaga Turkey Casserole with
        Gruyère-Broccoli Bread
        Crumbs, 130
    Spicy Butternut Squash Nachos,
        60–61
    Tuna Parsnip Portobello Melts,
        104–5, *105*
    Vegetarian Carrot Enchilada Bake,
        127–28, *129*

Cherries, Farro, Walnuts, and Goat
    Cheese, Pears with, *62, 63*
Chia Seed Lemon-Mint Dressing, 71
Chicken
    Avocado-Lime Mason Jar Salad,
        86–87, *87*
    Banh Mi with Sriracha Greek
        Yogurt, *108,* 109–10
    and Broccoli Skillet Bake, 137
    Carrot Noodle Soup, 76, *77*
    Kohlrabi and Sausage Breakfast
        Sauté with Spicy Salsa Verde,
        52–53
Chiles
    Albondigas and Chayote with
        Tomato-Serrano Sauce, *178,*
        179–80
    Vegan Chipotle Carrot Mac and
        Cheese, 131
Chili, Cajun Beef Celeriac, 79
Chimichurri, Seared Ahi Tuna with,
    186, 187
Chocolate
    Chip Sweet Potato Muffins, *206,* 207
    Double, –Pecan Sweet Potato
        Dessert Pancakes, 202–3
    Drizzle, Pecan and Carrot Almond
        Butter Bars with, *192,* 194
Cinnamon-Walnut Protein Muffins, 43
Clam Sauce, Garlic, Zucchini Linguine
    with, *172,* 173
Collard Hummus Wraps with Golden
    Beets and Sprouts, 111
Corn
    Avocado-Lime Mason Jar Salad,
        86–87, *87*
    Huevos Rancheros, *44,* 45–46
    Jícama, and Kiwi Salad with Honey-
        Mint Dressing, 88
    Spicy Butternut Squash Nachos,
        60–61
    -Tomato Salsa, 102–3
    Vegetarian Carrot Enchilada Bake,
        127–28, *129*
Crab, Spicy Garlic, with Parsnips, 171
Cucumber(s), 210
    Avocado, and Strawberry Salsa,
        58, *59*
    Beet Rice Nori Rolls with Chipotle-
        Teriyaki Sauce, 106, *107*
    Cauliflower Tabouleh Salad, *94,*
        95–96

Chicken Banh Mi with Sriracha
    Greek Yogurt, *108,* 109–10
Mango-Avocado Spring Rolls with
    Sriracha-Lime Dipping Sauce, 73
-Mint Raita, 66–67
Noodle Salad with Feta, Arugula,
    and Red Wine Vinaigrette, 97
Pork Bibimbap with Ginger
    Gochugaru, *150,* 151–52
Seared Ahi Tuna with Chimichurri,
    186, 187

D
Daikon (radish), 211
    Chicken Banh Mi with Sriracha
        Greek Yogurt, *108,* 109–10
    Pork Bibimbap with Ginger
        Gochugaru, *150,* 151–52
    Ramen with Skirt Steak, 80–81, *81*
    Shrimp Pho, 82
    for spiralized rice, 24
Dressings
    Honey-Mint, 88
    Honey-Pistachio Balsamic, 89
    Lemon-Mint Chia Seed, 71
    Red Wine Vinaigrette, 97

E
Egg(s)
    Chorizo and Avocado Zucchini
        Frittata with Manchego–Pea
        Shoot Salad, *36,* 36–37
    Drop Soup, Ginger Scallion, 78
    Ham and Rutabaga Breakfast
        Skillet, 42
    Huevos Rancheros, *44,* 45–46
    Kohlrabi and Sausage Breakfast
        Sauté with Spicy Salsa Verde,
        52–53
    Muffins, Pesto Sun-dried Tomato,
        38–39
    Pork Bibimbap with Ginger
        Gochugaru, *150,* 151–52
    Savoy Cabbage Breakfast Burrito,
        50, 51
    Sweet Potato Carbonara, 185
    Sweet Potato Fried Rice, 153
Endive Cups, Beet, Goat Cheese,
    and Pomegranate, 72, *72*

F
Farro, Cherries, Walnuts, and Goat
    Cheese, Pears with, *62, 63*
Fig, Pear, and Fontina Salad with
    Honey-Pistachio Balsamic, 89

INDEX   221

Fish. *See also* Shellfish
    Halibut en Papillote with Butternut
        Squash, 174, *175*
    Seared Ahi Tuna with Chimichurri,
        186, 187
    Spicy Seafood-Chorizo Paella, 154,
        155
    Teriyaki Salmon Balls with Ginger-
        Pineapple Rice, 147–48, *149*
    Tilapia Tostadas with Tomato-Corn
        Salsa, 102–3
    Tuna Parsnip Portobello Melts,
        104–5, *105*
Fruit. *See also specific fruits*
    best suited for spiralizing, 21–22
    noodles, best spiralizing methods,
        215–17
    noodles, yields and sizes, 214–15
    preparing, for spiralizing, 22–23

G
Garlic Lemon Broccoli with Bacon,
    64, 65
Ginger Scallion Egg Drop Soup, 78
Grape Leaves, Stuffed, Casserole,
    134–35, *135*

H
Halibut en Papillote with Butternut
    Squash, 174, *175*
Ham
    Balsamic Glazed Peaches with
        Prosciutto and Roquefort, *68,*
        69–70
    and Rutabaga Breakfast Skillet, 42
Honey
    -Mint Dressing, 88
    -Pistachio Balsamic, 89
Huevos Rancheros, *44, 45*–46
Hummus Collard Wraps with Golden
    Beets and Sprouts, 111

I
Ice Pops, Blueberry Pear, 204, *205*

J
Jícama, 210
    Kiwi, and Corn Salad with Honey-
        Mint Dressing, 88
    Rice, Coconut-Lime, Spicy Shrimp
        Lettuce Wraps with, 112–13, *113*
    for spiralized rice, 24
    Strings, Spicy, 56, *57*
    -Stuffed Peppers with Asiago, *156,*
        157–58

K
Kale
    Crispy, Blood Orange, and Honey
        Walnuts, Beet Pasta with,
        164–66, *165*
    and Parsnip Gratin, *132,* 133
    Salad, Steak and Pear, 83
Kiwi, Jícama, and Corn Salad with
    Honey-Mint Dressing, 88
Kohlrabi, 210
    and Apple Slaw with Lemon-Mint
        Chia Seed Dressing, 71
    Bowl, Sesame Almond Butter, 167
    Cilantro-Lime, Jalapeño Turkey
        Burgers with, 114–15
    and Sausage Breakfast Sauté with
        Spicy Salsa Verde, 52–53
    for spiralized rice, 24
    Vegetarian Chana Masala with,
        159–60, *161*

L
Lamb, Rack of, Mustard and Herb-
    Crusted, with "Couscous," *144,*
    145–46
Lemon
    Garlic Broccoli with Bacon, *64,* 65
    -Mint Chia Seed Dressing, 71
Lettuce
    Jícama, Kiwi, and Corn Salad with
        Honey-Mint Dressing, 88
    Wraps, Spicy Shrimp, with Coconut-
        Lime Jícama Rice, 112–13, *113*

M
Mango-Avocado Cucumber Spring
    Rolls with Sriracha-Lime Dipping
    Sauce, 73
Meat. *See* Beef; Lamb; Pork
Mint
    -Cucumber Raita, 66–67
    -Honey Dressing, 88
Miso, Tofu, –Tahini Carrot Bowl,
    190–91
Muffins
    Chocolate Chip Sweet Potato, *206,*
        207
    Cinnamon-Walnut Protein, 43
    Egg, Pesto Sun-dried Tomato,
        38–39
Mushrooms
    Tuna Parsnip Portobello Melts,
        104–5, *105*

N
Nachos, Spicy Butternut Squash,
    60–61
Noodles, pasta vs. vegetable, 16–17
Nori Rolls, Beet Rice, with Chipotle-
    Teriyaki Sauce, 106, *107*
Nuts. *See also* Pecan(s); Walnut(s)
    Apple and Pear Ricotta Parfaits with
        Pistachios, *200,* 201
    Vegan Chipotle Carrot Mac and
        Cheese, 131

O
Olive(s)
    Arugula, and Onion Sweet Potato
        Pizza Stacks, *116,* 117–18
    Avocado-Lime Mason Jar Salad,
        86–87, *87*
    Mediterranean Beet and Feta
        Skillet Bake, 122, *123*
    Vegetarian Carrot Enchilada Bake,
        127–28, *129*
Onion, 210
    Bhaji, Baked, with Mint-Cucumber
        Raita, 66–67
    Pickled, and Watermelon Salad with
        Ricotta Salata, *90,* 91
Orange, Blood, Honey Walnuts, and
    Crispy Kale, Beet Pasta with,
    164–66, *165*

P
Paella, Spicy Seafood-Chorizo, 154,
    155
Pancakes, Dessert, Double
    Chocolate–Pecan Sweet Potato,
    202–3
Parsnip(s), 211
    and Kale Gratin, *132,* 133
    Spicy Garlic Crab with, 171
    Tuna Portobello Melts, 104–5, *105*
Peaches, Balsamic Glazed, with
    Prosciutto and Roquefort, *68,*
    69–70
Pear(s), 211
    and Apple Ricotta Parfaits with
        Pistachios, *200,* 201
    Blueberry Ice Pops, 204, *205*
    with Farro, Cherries, Walnuts, and
        Goat Cheese, *62,* 63
    Fontina, and Fig Salad with
        Honey-Pistachio Balsamic, 89
    Rhubarb Crisp, 195
    and Steak Kale Salad, 83

Peas
     Spicy Seafood-Chorizo Paella, 154,
          155
     Sweet Potato Fried Rice, 153
Pecan(s)
     Apple Ambrosia Fruit Salad, 196, *197*
     and Carrot Almond Butter Bars with
          Chocolate Drizzle, *192*, 194
     –Double Chocolate Sweet Potato
          Dessert Pancakes, 202–3
     Shaved Asparagus, and
          Gorgonzola, Apples with, 92, *93*
Peppers. *See also* Chiles
     Avocado-Lime Mason Jar Salad,
          86–87, *87*
     Chicken Banh Mi with Sriracha
          Greek Yogurt, *108*, 109–10
     Jícama-Stuffed, with Asiago, *156*,
          157–58
     Pesto Spaghetti with Heirloom
          Grape Tomatoes, 170
     Pesto Sun-dried Tomato Egg Muffins,
          38–39
     Pesto Turnips with Shredded
          Brussels Sprouts, *188*, 189
Pineapple
     Apple Ambrosia Fruit Salad, 196,
          197
     -Ginger Rice, Teriyaki Salmon Balls
          with, 147–48, *149*
Pistachios, Apple and Pear Ricotta
     Parfaits with, *200*, 201
Plantain(s), 211
     Cacao Balls, No-Bake, 198
     Coconut Rice Pudding, 199
     Huevos Rancheros, *44*, 45–46
     for spiralized rice, 24
     Tilapia Tostadas with Tomato-Corn
          Salsa, 102–3
Pomegranate, Beet, and Goat
     Cheese Endive Cups, 72, *72*
Pork. *See also* Bacon; Ham
     Bibimbap with Ginger Gochugaru,
          150, 151–52
     Chorizo and Avocado Zucchini
          Frittata with Manchego–Pea
          Shoot Salad, *36*, 36–37
     Fennel Sausage and Butternut
          Squash Casserole, 136
     Spicy Seafood-Chorizo Paella, 154,
          155
     Thai Drunken Zucchini Noodles
          with, 181

Potato(es), 211. *See also* Sweet
     Potato(es)
     -Apple Cheese Bun, 119
     "Everything Bagel" Breakfast Bun,
          47–48, *49*
     Pesto Sun-dried Tomato Egg
          Muffins, 38–39
Poultry. *See* Chicken; Turkey
Prosciutto and Roquefort, Balsamic
     Glazed Peaches with, *68*, 69–70
Pudding, Plantain Coconut Rice,
     199

Q
Quinoa
     Beet Superfood Bowl, 140, *141*
R
Radishes, 211
Rhubarb Pear Crisp, 195
Rice, spiralized, preparing, 24–25
Rutabaga, 211
     and Ham Breakfast Skillet, 42
     for spiralized rice, 24
     Turkey Casserole with Gruyère-
          Broccoli Bread Crumbs, 130

S
Salads
     Apple Ambrosia Fruit, 196, *197*
     Apple and Kohlrabi Slaw with
          Lemon-Mint Chia Seed
          Dressing, 71
     Apples with Shaved Asparagus,
          Gorgonzola, and Pecans, 92, *93*
     Avocado-Lime Mason Jar, 86–87, *87*
     Caprese Zucchini, *84*, 85
     Cauliflower Tabouleh, *94*, 95–96
     Cucumber Noodle, with Feta,
          Arugula, and Red Wine
          Vinaigrette, 97
     Jícama, Kiwi, and Corn, with Honey-
          Mint Dressing, 88
     Pear, Fontina, and Fig, with Honey-
          Pistachio Balsamic, 89
     Pickled Onion and Watermelon,
          with Ricotta Salata, 90, 91
     Steak and Pear Kale, 83
     Zucchini Pasta, Italian, 98, *99*
Salmon Balls, Teriyaki, with Ginger-
     Pineapple Rice, 147–48, *149*
Salsa
     Cucumber, Avocado, and
          Strawberry, 58, *59*
     Tomato-Corn, 102–3

Sandwiches
     Chicken Banh Mi with Sriracha
          Greek Yogurt, *108*, 109–10
     Collard Hummus Wraps with
          Golden Beets and Sprouts, 111
Sausage(s)
     Chorizo and Avocado Zucchini
          Frittata with Manchego–Pea
          Shoot Salad, *36*, 36–37
     Fennel, and Butternut Squash
          Casserole, 136
     and Kohlrabi Breakfast Sauté with
          Spicy Salsa Verde, 52–53
     Spicy Seafood-Chorizo Paella, 154,
          155
Seafood. *See* Fish; Shellfish
Sesame Almond Butter Kohlrabi
     Bowl, 167
Shellfish
     Shrimp Daikon Pho, 82
     Spicy Garlic Crab with Parsnips,
          171
     Spicy Seafood-Chorizo Paella,
          154, *155*
     Spicy Shrimp Lettuce Wraps with
          Coconut-Lime Jícama Rice,
          112–13, *113*
     Zucchini Linguine with Garlic Clam
          Sauce, *172*, 173
Shrimp
     Daikon Pho, 82
     Lettuce Wraps, Spicy, with
          Coconut-Lime Jícama Rice,
          112–13, *113*
     Spicy Seafood-Chorizo Paella, 154,
          155
Slaw, Apple and Kohlrabi, with
     Lemon-Mint Chia Seed
     Dressing, 71
Soups
     Chicken Carrot Noodle, 76, *77*
     Ginger Scallion Egg Drop, 78
     Shrimp Daikon Pho, 82
Spinach
     Beet Superfood Bowl, 140, *141*
     Deconstructed Zucchini Manicotti,
          124, 125–26
     Pesto Sun-dried Tomato Egg
          Muffins, 38–39
     Pork Bibimbap with Ginger
          Gochugaru, *150*, 151–52

Spiralizing
    choosing blade for, 23–24
    choosing foods for, 21–22
    kitchen tools for, 29
    pantry ingredients for, 29–31
    preparing food for, 22–23
    recipe features, 29
    tips and tricks, 27–29
Spring Rolls, Mango-Avocado
    Cucumber, with Sriracha-Lime
    Dipping Sauce, 73
Squash. *See also* Zucchini
    butternut, 209
    Butternut, and Fennel Sausage
        Casserole, 136
    Butternut, Halibut en Papillote with,
        174, *175*
    Butternut, Nachos, Spicy, 60–61
    for spiralized rice, 24
    summer, 212
Strawberry, Cucumber, and Avocado
    Salsa, 58, *59*
Sweet Potato(es), 212
    Blueberry Waffles, 40, *41*
    Carbonara, 185
    Chocolate Chip Muffins, *206*, 207
    Cinnamon-Walnut Protein Muffins,
        43
    Dessert Pancakes, Double
        Chocolate–Pecan, 202–3
    Fried Rice, 153
    "Grits," Short Ribs with, 142
    Pizza Stacks, Arugula, Olive, and
        Onion, *116*, 117–18
    Savoy Cabbage Breakfast Burrito,
        50, 51
    for spiralized rice, 24

T

Tilapia Tostadas with Tomato-Corn
    Salsa, 102–3
Tofu Miso–Tahini Carrot Bowl, 190–91
Tomato(es)
    Bikini Bolognese, 176–77
    Caprese Zucchini Salad, *84*, 85
    -Corn Salsa, 102–3
    Deconstructed Zucchini Manicotti,
        124, 125–26

Heirloom Grape, Pesto Spaghetti
    with, 170
Italian Zucchini Pasta Salad, 98, *99*
Mediterranean Beet and Feta
    Skillet Bake, 122, *123*
-Serrano Sauce, Albondigas and
    Chayote with, *178*, 179–80
Spicy Butternut Squash Nachos,
    60–61
Tomatokeftedes and Cauliflower
    Tabouleh Salad, *94*, 95–96
Vegetarian Chana Masala with
    Kohlrabi, 159–60, *161*
Tostadas, Tilapia, with Tomato-Corn
    Salsa, 102–3
Tuna
    Ahi, Seared, with Chimichurri, *186*,
        187
    Parsnip Portobello Melts, 104–5,
        105
Turkey
    Bikini Bolognese, 176–77
    Jalapeño, Burgers with Cilantro-
        Lime Kohlrabi, 114–15
    Rutabaga Casserole with Gruyère-
        Broccoli Bread Crumbs, 130
Turnips, 212
    Mustard and Herb-Crusted Rack
        of Lamb with "Couscous," *144*,
        145–46
    Pesto, with Shredded Brussels
        Sprouts, *188*, 189
    for spiralized rice, 24

V

Vegetable(s). *See also specific*
    vegetables
    best suited for spiralizing, 21–22
    health benefits, 15–16
    noodles, best spiralizing methods,
        215–17
    noodles, nutritional information,
        214
    noodles, vs. regular noodles, 16–17
    noodles, yields and sizes, 214–15
    preparing, for spiralizing, 22–23
    recommended daily intake, 17
    spiralized, storing, 28–29

W

Waffles, Blueberry Sweet Potato,
    40, *41*
Walnut(s)
    -Cinnamon Protein Muffins, 43
    Farro, Cherries, and Goat Cheese,
        Pears with, 62, *63*
    Fennel Sausage and Butternut
        Squash Casserole, 136
    Honey, Blood Orange, and Crispy
        Kale, Beet Pasta with, 164–66,
        165
Watermelon and Pickled Onion Salad
    with Ricotta Salata, *90*, 91

Y

Yogurt
    Blueberry Pear Ice Pops, 204, *205*
    Greek, Sriracha, Chicken Banh Mi
        with, *108*, 109–10
    Mint-Cucumber Raita, 66–67
    Tzatziki, *94*, 95–96
Yuca or cassava root, 212

Z

Zucchini, 212
    Avocado-Lime Mason Jar Salad,
        86–87, *87*
    Bacon Cacio e Pepe, 168, *169*
    Balsamic Glazed Peaches with
        Prosciutto and Roquefort, *68*,
        69–70
    Bikini Bolognese, 176–77
    Frittata, Chorizo and Avocado, with
        Manchego–Pea Shoot Salad,
        36, 36–37
    Ginger Scallion Egg Drop Soup, 78
    Linguine with Garlic Clam Sauce,
        172, 173
    Manicotti, Deconstructed, *124*,
        125–26
    noodles, saucing, 27
    Noodles, Thai Drunken, with Pork,
        181
    Pasta Salad, Italian, 98, *99*
    Pesto Spaghetti with Heirloom
        Grape Tomatoes, 170
    Salad, Caprese, *84*, 85
    for spiralized rice, 24